T0347379

The Economics of Small Firms

In recent years, the economic analysis of new and small firms has grown rapidly. As a result, the theoretical and empirical literature is now extensive. The sheer scale and technical nature of this literature means that much of it is beyond the reach of the substantial numbers of students at both undergraduate and postgraduate levels who are now taking courses in business and management and related subjects.

This important new text provides a condensed but rounded introduction to small business economics for those who may have only an elementary knowledge of economics. Economics, alongside other disciplines and interacting with them, has some important insights to offer and it is in this context that *The Economics of Small Firms* examines the formation, survival, growth and financing of small businesses, spatial variations in business formation, the economic role of small businesses and key policy issues. It will be an essential purchase for anybody studying business and management and eager for an accessible and engaging overview of economics and entrepreneurship and small business.

Peter Johnson is Emeritus Professor of Business Economics in the Centre for Entrepreneurship at Durham University. He has published a wide range of studies on new and small firms. He has also taught small business economics at undergraduate and postgraduate levels.

The Economics of Small Firms

An introduction

Peter Johnson

Routledge
Taylor & Francis Group

LONDON AND NEW YORK

First published 2007
by Routledge
2 Park Square, Milton Park, Abingdon, Oxon OX14 4RN

Simultaneously published in the USA and Canada
by Routledge
270 Madison Avenue, New York, NY 10016

Routledge is an imprint of the Taylor & Francis Group, an informa business

Typeset in Garamond
by Keystroke, 28 High Street, Tettenhall, Wolverhampton
Printed and bound in Great Britain
by TJ International Ltd, Padstow, Cornwall

British Library Cataloguing in Publication Data
A catalogue record for this book is available from the British Library

Library of Congress Cataloging in Publication Data
A catalog record for this book has been requested
Johnson, P. S.
The economics of small firms : an introduction / Peter Johnson.
p. cm.
Includes bibliographical references and index.
ISBN 0–415–39337–X (hard cover) – ISBN 0–415–39338–8 (soft cover)
1. Small business. 2. Small business–Finance. I. Title.
HD2341.J64 2007
338.6´42–dc22   2006032124

ISBN10: 0–415–39337–X (hbk)
ISBN10: 0–415–39338–8 (pbk)

ISBN13: 978–0–415–39337–9 (hbk)
ISBN13: 978–0–415–39338–6 (pbk)

Contents

Illustrations

Preface

In recent years, the economic analysis of new and small firms has grown very rapidly. As a result, the theoretical and empirical literature is now extensive. The sheer scale and technical nature of this literature mean that much of it is beyond the reach of the substantial numbers of students at both undergraduate and postgraduate levels who are now taking courses in small businesses management and related subjects. Many of these students have studied economics only at introductory level; relatively few have gone any further. This book has been written with these students in mind and in a firm belief that economics, alongside other disciplines and interacting with them, has some important insights to offer, in terms of both approach and substantive findings.

While the book draws extensively on the economic literature, it does so in a way that makes this literature intelligible to the non-specialist. Some appreciation of elementary supply and demand analysis is taken as given, particularly in Chapter 8, but little other knowledge of formal economic analysis is assumed. I briefly outline the concept of minimum efficient scale at the end of Chapter 2, because this concept is particularly helpful when looking at the efficiency of small firm operation.

This is not a hands-on 'how to do it' book, but I would like to think that there is much here that would help the would-be or existing small businessman or businesswoman (see Chapter 10). In particular it should provide a bigger context for their thinking. The book should also be of interest to postgraduate researchers and policymakers who are seeking a fairly condensed but rounded introduction to small business economics.

Acknowledgements

I owe a substantial debt of gratitude to the generations of students who have enrolled on the small business economics courses that I have run over the years. Their comments and questions have been an enormous help in writing this book. It has also been good to have academic colleagues at Durham and elsewhere who have interests in self-employment, entrepreneurship, small business and related topics and who have contributed (often unknowingly) to some of the thinking in this book. At Durham, Simon Parker, John Ritchie, Martin Robson, Paul Robson, Ian Stone, Philip Vale and Frits Wijbenga have been especially helpful. Further afield, it has been good to discuss ideas with David Storey at Warwick, Andrew Burke at Cranfield, Mark Hart at Kingston and Colin Mason at Strathclyde. Lynne Evans and Paul Robson kindly read and commented on particular chapters. None of these people of course bears any responsibility for the contents of this book.

Blackwell Publishing kindly granted me permission to use material in Chapter 5 from an article of mine that first appeared in *Entrepreneurship Theory and Practice*. I am also grateful to: Maria Minniti and her colleagues in the *GEM* Consortium for permission to use some data in Table 5.1; the Bank of England for permission to reproduce the quotation on p. 105; Ian Dale and Trends Business Research, Newcastle, for allowing me to utilise their data in Table 7.3; and EIM Business and Policy Research, Brussels, who gave permission for me to use data originally provided by them to the European Commission. Crown copyright material has been used under PSI Licence no. C2006009473. I have endeavoured to give full acknowledgement of sources.

Last but not least, I should like to thank my wife, Barbara, for her whole-hearted support throughout the project.

Abbreviations

BVCA	British Venture Capital Association
DTI	Department of Trade and Industry
EPL	employment protection legislation
ESEA	early-stage entrepreneurial activity
GDP	gross domestic product
GEM	*Global Entrepreneurship Monitor*
GNP	gross national product
ICC	industrial composition component
ICFC	Industrial and Commercial Finance Corporation
LPE	Law of Proportionate Effect
LRAC	long run average cost
MES	minimum efficient scale
NCDS	National Child Development Study
OECD	Organization for Economic Cooperation and Development
PV	present value
RDA	Regional Development Agency
RPI	Retail Prices Index
SEDA	South East Development Agency
SFLGS	Small Firms Loan Guarantee Scheme
SFSC	small firm share component
SMEs	small and medium-sized enterprises
TBSF	technology-based small firms
VAT	Value Added Tax

1 Introduction

Policy interest in small firms

Since the early 1970s there has been a very substantial increase in policy interest in the economic role of the small firm. This growth in interest has been worldwide. Governments in advanced economies have increasingly attributed key economic roles to such firms – employment generation, the development and introduction of new and improved products and processes, and the maintenance and enhancement of competitive forces. Entrepreneurial activity is seen as being channelled principally through new and small firms. The question of whether or not such views are justified is addressed at various points in this book.

The development of government policies towards small firms has reflected numerous factors including a more positive social culture and economic environment for entrepreneurship and self-employment, and changes in demand and technology. How far government policies have driven such developments, and how far they have simply reacted to them, is however a question that must remain open.

A further stimulus to policy interest in the economic role of small firms in recent decades was the collapse of Communism in Eastern Europe and the move by the countries involved towards more market-based economies. The consequent privatisation of state industries, and the search for employment opportunities for workers made redundant as a result, have focused attention on how best to encourage indigenous industry. The development of new, home-grown, small firms is one obvious route for developing such industry.

In developing economies, the activities of small firms have long received a good deal of attention, since such firms, typically consisting of a single individual or family, have traditionally been the dominant form of productive organisation. But the increased focus on small firms in developed economies has further stimulated this concern.

The growth in interest in small firms in the policy arena has been matched in the academic field. In the United Kingdom for example, there is now a multitude of courses, offered at all levels, on entrepreneurship and the management of new and small business. Numerous research centres devoted to the analysis of small firms and the problems and opportunities they face, have been set up. Many university chairs in the subject have been established. There are now several well-established journals in the small firms area.

Academic work on small firms

Academic work on small firms has been carried out in a variety of disciplines, notably business management, economics, geography and sociology. Research has benefited from the different perspectives that these disciplines have brought to the task. Economists were perhaps the slowest to get off the mark in making a contribution to the understanding of small business. The reasons for this tardiness are not difficult to find. Up to the late 1960s and early 1970s, a key preoccupation of industrial economists was the existence and benefits of economies of large scale, in both production and technology, and little attention was given to the benefits that small operations might bring.[1] Furthermore, microeconomic theory characterised the small firm operating in an atomistic market as essentially a passive responder to its economic environment. These firms were perceived as having no distinguishing features worthy of investigation: each firm is forced into a uniform mould by the rigours of competition; any firm not conforming to that mould is forced out of business. And there was little room for entrepreneurial drive and activity in a world where economic actors were assumed to have full information.

Fortunately, the interest of economists in small firms has increased very substantially in recent years, and there have been many important contributions to the literature. This increased interest was reflected in, and further stimulated by, the launch, in 1989, of *Small Business Economics*, the first journal specifically devoted to small firm economics. There is however still much to do, and the following chapters will highlight some of the main gaps that remain.

Plan and purpose of the book

The purpose of this book is to provide an introduction to the economics of small business that is accessible to those whose economics training is limited. The book covers both theoretical and empirical issues. In Chapter 2 the justification for examining small firms is explored. This chapter also considers some basic international data on the importance of small firms. As the notion of entrepreneurship is often closely linked to small firms, Chapter 3 explores the contributions made by economists to the understanding of the entrepreneurial function. It also examines the implications of these contributions for the analysis of small firms' activity.

In Chapter 4 the focus is on the formation decision and the factors affecting it. Chapter 5 builds on this discussion with an examination of variations in formation rates across countries and regions. This chapter also draws on research into variations in these rates over time and across industries. It is of course one thing to form a business, and quite another to survive or to grow. Chapter 6 considers some of the factors that affect the survival rate and the growth of new businesses. It also looks at the determinants of small firm growth more generally. As part of this exercise, the various attempts that have been made to categorise entrepreneurs and owners are considered.

Chapter 7 examines some key aspects of the economic impact of new and small businesses. The contribution of these businesses to employment generation, their role in innovation, the ways in which they influence competition and their contribution to economic growth are considered.

Finance for small firms is already the subject of a substantial literature. It is therefore considered as a topic in its own right in Chapter 8. As financial support for small firms has been a key element in policy, this chapter forms a good basis for looking at the broader policy issues in Chapter 9. The book concludes, in Chapter 10, with some reflections on the implications of the economic analysis of small firms for their management.

Although there is a fairly strong bias towards UK material in this book, especially when it comes to some of the descriptive material, the underlying issues that are addressed have much wider application. Use has also been made, where appropriate, of European Union (EU) and US studies and data.

There are of course a number of excellent texts that deal with some of the ground covered here. David Storey's (1994) text is outstanding in this field but is now looking a little dated. Several management texts on small business – a good example is Paul Burns' (2007) comprehensive volume – inevitably draw on economic concepts and evidence. However, the primary focus of these books is elsewhere. There are also some important collections of readings and studies.[2] These constitute an invaluable source of reference but for most students, they offer too much detail and depth.

2 Why study small firms?

Introduction

Why study small firms? One obvious reason is that these firms account for nearly all firms in most advanced countries. For example, firms of fewer than ten employees ('micro enterprises' in the official EU jargon: see Table 2.2 on p. 9) represent about 92 per cent of all firms in the non- agricultural sectors of 'Europe-19' countries (Table 2.3 on p. 11).[1] This rises to 99 per cent if the upper limit for the number of employees is raised to forty-nine (micro plus 'small' enterprises). Thus if the focus of interest is on explaining firm behaviour, it makes sense to concentrate on these businesses. Firms at the lower end of the size distribution do of course account for a much smaller proportion of (say) total employment or sales, because of the presence of a few very large firms. Even when these yardsticks are used however, they remain significant: for example, Europe-19 micro enterprises have a share of about 39 per cent of total employment.

The actual number of micro and small enterprises is very substantial. The data in Table 2.3 suggest that there were over 19 million such businesses in the Europe-19 countries in 2003. Even this figure may be a significant underestimate.[2] The European Commission (2004: 33) estimated that the figure for the United States was in the order of 21 million.

In addition to numerical significance, a number of important economic functions have been attributed to the small firm. They are widely seen as important generators of jobs, and as significant conduits for innovation and productivity growth, topics that are considered in more detail in later chapters. Small firms, through their role as a competitive 'fringe', may also have a part to play in restricting the ability of dominant firms to exploit their existing market positions (see Chapter 7).

Furthermore, a few small firms may grow to a significant size, and eventually challenge the current generation of large firms. It is important to acknowledge however that this typically takes considerable time. For example, the Sainsbury Group, which in 2005 had a turnover of £16.4 billion, and employed around 153,000 people, has taken well over 130 years to reach its current position, starting out life as a single shop in Drury Lane, London at the end of the 1860s

(Williams 1994). Some of today's major businesses developed in a far shorter time – Microsoft for example was founded in 1975 and Body Shop in 1976 – but these are the exception. Whatever the time span involved, it still remains relatively rare for a small firm to develop into a major corporation. At the same time, it is salutary to remember that virtually all of today's giants can be traced back to very small beginnings. This 'seedbed' role of the small firm sector is considered in Chapter 7.

Another reason for examining small firms is that they may have distinctive business characteristics in relation to management style, ownership patterns and product range, that make it logical for them to be studied as a separate group. Most small firms for example may be classified as family businesses; as Chapter 6 shows, such businesses face particular challenges.

Finally, small firms may raise distinctive policy issues. For example, it is frequently argued these firms experience various forms of disadvantage as a result of their size. Compliance with taxation requirements, safety and employment legislation are all instances where diseconomies of small size may be experienced as a result of the presence of significant 'fixed' costs. The policy issue here is whether firms that are disadvantaged in this way should receive assistance from the state to compensate. This proposition is considered further in Chapter 9. It is sufficient to note here that even if some of these arguments for intervention are valid, it does not automatically follow that *efficient* policies can be devised to offset the inherent disadvantage of being small.

A number of possible justifications for looking at small firms has been suggested above. It should however be stressed that much of the case for singling out small firms for separate study rests on their distinctiveness *relative to firms of other sizes*. For example, as far as the contribution of small firms to innovation is concerned, it is important, both for policy reasons and for an understanding of business behaviour, to show that this contribution *differs* in some way from that of large firms. Such comparisons can be made only if the whole size range is studied, and the effects of *scale* on business activities and characteristics are examined. This is not simply an academic point. It is often unclear from empirical research on small firms whether the reported results are distinctive to a particular size category. For example the Acs and Audretsch (1988) study – see pp. 93–4 – on firm size and innovation is based on a single break point of 500 employees, but it is unclear how the results might change if different size boundaries were used.

It should also be pointed out that some of the interest in small firms arises because the lower end of the size distribution is likely to include the most recently formed firms, some of which will rapidly grow out of their initial size band. Firm age and firm size are likely to have different impacts on the way in which firms behave and on their economic contribution. Disentangling the effects is however difficult.

Some definitional issues

Defining the boundaries of the firm

So far two important definitional questions over small firms have been conveniently sidestepped. The first of these questions is: what is a 'firm' (or 'enterprise' or 'business')? The second is: what is meant by 'small'? The first opens up a range of issues relating to the nature of the firm, a topic on which there is a huge literature.[3] This literature lies largely outside the remit of this book. The main focus here will simply be on legally independent trading organisations. Firms which in legal terms are subsidiaries of other businesses are not considered.

While the emphasis on legally independent traders is convenient in that it provides a useful practical test for delineating firm boundaries, it nevertheless throws up some potential difficulties. One of these is that ostensibly legally independent organisations may sometimes be heavily dependent on other similar organisations. For example, a self-employed tenant of a public house would, under the definition adopted here, be regarded as a firm, even though such an individual is wholly dependent on his or her landlord for supplies, and may have to conform to a wide variety of detailed requirements about the pub's operations. In franchise arrangements, similarly, the franchisee is often very heavily constrained in relation to what he or she can or cannot do by the agreement with the franchisor. Even where there are no franchise agreements, an organisation which meets the legal independence criterion may still be heavily dependent for its supplies and/or its sales on another firm.[4]

There is another aspect of the relationships between seemingly independent firms that should be noted. A focus on *legal* aspects of independence only, ignores the often very complex family, social and personal ties that frequently exist between businesses. For example, a husband and wife may run separate businesses, but their relationship may have a fundamental effect on how the businesses interact with each other. Wider family ties may also link businesses: Scherer and Ross (1990: 64) for example point out that in the 1960s, eight of the ten largest private sector manufacturers in Sweden were effectively controlled by one family. Membership of the same clubs and societies may provide a further mechanism for business owners to coordinate their activities.

Many small firms are part of well-established informal networks of business relationships involving suppliers, buyers and others working in similar markets. These networks often provide mutual support and enable the sharing of experience – a function that is not well reflected in the notion of legal independence. Another complication arises in the corporate sector as a result of interlocking directorates (Johnson and Apps 1979; Scherer and Ross 1990: 67–8) where companies have common directors.

All these links between businesses suggest that the narrow concept of legal independence may be much less significant in terms of the way in which business activity is conducted and managed, than standard textbook treatments of the firm sometimes imply. This is likely to be at least as true for the small firm sector, as it is for large firms. The complex – and often messy – nature of relationships *between* small firms cannot be ignored if the role of such firms is to be comprehensively analysed. Indeed, for this reason, it might make sense, for some purposes, to use the *network* as the unit of analysis rather than the individual firm. At the same time, the legally independent firm still represents a key focus for economic activity and policy, and it is this unit that is the primary concern in this book.

Measuring 'smallness'

The measurement of smallness raises at least two issues. The first concerns the choice of yardstick. Absolute size or market size, i.e. a relative measure, may be chosen as the criterion. The second of these yardsticks in turn requires the appropriate market boundaries to be defined. In either case, the precise metric then has to be decided. Employment, sales and assets are obvious possibilities here, but they often give different indications of the relative importance of small firms. Small firms tend to be less capital intensive than their larger counterparts (see pp. 11–12). The second issue is the choice of a dividing line between 'small' and other size categories. How these measurement issues are resolved has important implications for market rankings in terms of the importance of small firms, for the analysis of small firm activities and for policy formulation.

One way of tackling the dividing line issue is first to define some economically distinctive features of the small firm, and then to translate this into some statistical counterpart. It is this 'economic characteristics' approach which was adopted in the United Kingdom in the seminal report of the Bolton Committee of Inquiry on Small Firms (1971). This report, published in the early 1970s, is still the best starting point for a consideration of definitional issues.

The Bolton Committee (1971: para 1.4) identified three distinguishing characteristics:

1   *A small firm is one that has a relatively small share of the market.* 'Relatively small' does of course itself need to be defined. The Bolton Committee (1971) had in mind a market share which meant that the firm lacked any 'real power to affect its environment' (para 1.5). Such a characteristic clearly fits many businesses that are absolutely small. However it should be remembered that in some cases even one-person operations may have significant market power, where for example they occupy a market niche. Some software firms generating highly specialist applications in very narrowly defined areas, such as in the oil industry, may come into this category. By the same token, substantial businesses may operate in a highly competitive environment, especially when the market is defined most appropriately in international terms. Dominance of the UK market may not provide much protection against international competition.

2 *A small firm is one that is managed by its owners or part-owners in a personalised way.* Thus the owners are active participants in 'all aspects of the management' of the firm, and take 'all the principal decisions' (para 1.6).

3 *A small firm is independent.* It is not part of other larger enterprises, and the owner is free from outside control in taking the main decisions. It is clear that the Bolton Committee had in mind here *legal* independence.

Having suggested some basic economic characteristics, the Bolton Committee then proceeded to translate these characteristics into statistical counterparts. It took the view that different types of measure were appropriate for different sectors.[5] In manufacturing, the Bolton Committee set an upper limit of 200 employees, arguing that the vast majority of firms coming within this definition conformed to its economic criteria. It is however difficult to see how a firm of 200 employees could meet the second of Bolton's economic criteria: by the time a firm has reached this size, it is unlikely to be under the personalised control of the owners.

In non-manufacturing, the application of the same employment criterion would define as 'small' some businesses that, relative to the industry in which they operated, would be regarded as very substantial. In these sectors, the Bolton Committee applied 'a series of more or less arbitrary definitions in terms of whatever measures appear[ed] appropriate' (1971: para 1.9).

Table 2.1 sets out the original definitions and has updated the financial yardsticks to 2006 prices using the Retail Prices Index (RPI). It should be noted that this updating of the financial measures used by Bolton and the non-updating of the physical measures have not allowed for the possibility

Table 2.1 Small firms: some definitions

Sector	Bolton definition, 1971	Equivalent in 2006[a]
Manufacturing	200 employees or fewer	200 employees or fewer
Retailing	£50,000 turnover or less	£487,000 or less
Wholesaling	£200,000 turnover or less	£1,947,000 or less
Construction	25 employees or fewer	25 employees or fewer
Mining/quarrying	25 employees or fewer	25 employees or fewer
Motor trades	£100,000 turnover or less	£974,000 or less
Misc. services	£50,000 turnover or less	£487,000 or less
Road transport	5 vehicles or fewer	5 vehicles or fewer
Catering	All excluding multiples and brewery-managed public houses	All excluding multiples and brewery-managed public houses

Source: Bolton Committee (1971: 3); www.statistics.gov.uk.

Note: [a] The turnover figures have been adjusted by the RPI (all items) index.

that the 'technology' of management may have changed in such a way that, for example, personalised control – see point 2 above – can now be maintained over a wider area of business.

Table 2.1 highlights the diversity of measures used by Bolton. While this diversity has some strengths, it also makes comparisons across industrial sectors rather difficult.

Since Bolton, attention has tended increasingly to focus on small and medium-sized enterprises (SMEs). In 2005, the European Commission adopted the broad enterprise size classes provided in Table 2.2. Alongside the size criteria, an SME must meet at least one financial test, together with an independence criterion: no other business or linked businesses must have more than a 25 per cent ownership stake.

It is not at all clear what underlying economic rationale exists for this breakdown. While it is true, as Storey (1994: 13) has pointed out, that the dividing line between 'very small' (or 'micro') and 'small' has some economic justification in that it roughly corresponds to the point where a firm tends to develop a more formal management structure, it is far less obvious why the other size boundaries are located where they are. Indeed the Commission has itself changed these boundaries significantly in recent years. In its 1990 report on *Enterprises in the European Community* (Commission of the European Communities 1990: 2.3), the Commission placed the border between 'small' and 'medium' at 100 employees, and between 'medium' and 'large' at 500. The justification for the move to the current, very different, headcount classification is not immediately apparent. It is also worth noting that in the mid-1990s, the Commission adopted a recommendation that yet further amended its definition of SMEs and introduced the independence requirement.[6] It is perhaps inevitable that as a statistical database develops, there will be definitional changes. At the same time however, the significant realignment of enterprise size categories and the

Table 2.2 European Commission SME definitions from 2005

Category	Headcount	Turnover[a]	Assets[a]	Independence
Micro enterprises	<10	≤ €2mn	≤ €2mn	Not more than 25% owned by another enterprise or other enterprises linked to one another[b]
Small enterprises	<50	≤ €10mn	≤ €10mn	
Micro, small and medium-sized enterprises	<250	≤ €50mn	≤ €43mn	
Large enterprises	≥250	> €50mn	> €43mn	

Source: Derived from the *Official Journal of the European Union*, 20 May 2003, L124, vol. 46.

Notes: [a] The enterprise has to satisfy at least one of these conditions.
[b] The detailed conditions for independence are complex: see the source above.

introduction of additional criteria suggest some uncertainty about the underlying principles that should be applied.

A number of other approaches to small firm definition have been suggested. For example, some researchers (e.g. Curran and Blackburn 2001: 17) have derived definitions that are 'grounded' in a consensus developed by the businesses and industry concerned. Such an approach may of course lead to significant variations across industries. It is also likely to be costly in terms of data collection.

In one sense of course definitional matters are not terribly important. It is simply necessary to define the small firm in a way which is appropriate for the task in hand. For some research tasks, it may not even be appropriate to define such a firm. If for example, the focus of interest is on the effects of *scale* on various firm performance measures, or on the impact of economic influences on scale, then it makes sense to look across the whole size spectrum. However the definitional issue does take on greater significance where policy measures designed to benefit particular size categories of firm are introduced. This issue is further discussed in Chapter 9.

There is one final, but nevertheless important point that needs to be made in respect of small firm definitions: while the grouping of firms into size bands may be necessary for a range of purposes, there may still be very considerable heterogeneity, in terms of firm characteristics and performance *within* those bands. The grouping together of (say) a high tech university spin-off with a self-employed jobbing gardener because they are the same size, may make some sense, but the differences in owner, business and environmental characteristics are likely to be greater than any similarities deriving from their scale.

Throughout this book, the word 'small' will be used loosely to cover firms towards the lower end of the size distribution. The term 'SMEs' indicates a wider size spectrum. The context will sometimes make it clear precisely how these terms should be interpreted in statistical terms. Such a fluid usage reflects the nature of the literature.

Some summary data

In order to set the context for the rest of this book, some summary data on SMEs in Europe and elsewhere are presented below. The main purpose of the tabulations here is to provide some broad, descriptive feel for the scale of SME activity, without at this stage offering any evaluation.

In Table 2.3, some data on enterprise size in Europe-19 countries are presented. These data, which exclude agriculture and fishing, must be treated cautiously, as some estimation is involved. The table shows that virtually all enterprises are within the current SME definition although they account for a much smaller proportion (about 70 per cent) of employment. The table also demonstrates how average turnover per enterprise and value added per enterprise increase as the size category increases. Not surprisingly, the smaller the business, the lower the value added per occupied person tends to be. This latter

Table 2.3 Enterprises in Europe-19 by size category (non-agricultural market sectors), 2003

Measure	Size category				Total
	Micro	Small	Medium	Large	
Numbers (% of total numbers)	92.3	6.5	0.9	0.2	100.0 (19,310,000)
Employment (% of total employment)	39.4	17.4	13.0	30.3	100.0 (139,710,000)
Turnover per enterprise (1000 Euros)	440	3,610	25,680	319,020	1,550
Share of exports in turnover (%)	9	13	17	23	17
Value added per enterprise (1000 Euros)	120	1,180	8,860	126,030	540
Value added per occupied person (1000 Euros)	40	60	90	120	75
Share of labour costs in value added (%)	57	57	55	47	52

Source: Derived from European Commission (2004: 26). Estimated by EIM Business & Policy Research; estimates based on Eurostat's Structural Business Statistics and Eurostat's SME Database; also based on *European Economy*, Supplement A, May 2003, and *OECD: Economic Outlook*, no. 71, June 2003; due to rounding, totals may differ slightly from constituent parts.

finding reflects, in part at least, the higher capital intensity in large enterprises – reflected in the lower share of labour costs in value added (bottom row). It is also worth noting that the larger the enterprise, the higher the proportion of turnover coming from exports.

The summary nature of the data disguises significant variations in the relative importance of SMEs, both across both countries and industries. For example, the share of SMEs in employment in EU countries varies from 59 per cent (in the United Kingdom) to 87 per cent (in Greece): see Table 2.4. And as Table 2.5 illustrates, *sectors* vary in the extent to which they are dominated by the different size categories. The country and industry variations are related: at least some of the country variation may be explained by differences in industry mix.

Comparable data for other countries are not easily obtainable. However data for the United States (in 2000) and for Japan (in 2001) (European Commission 2004: 33) suggest that while both countries have a very similar proportion

Table 2.4 Employment share of SMEs in Europe-19 by country (non-agricultural market sectors), 2003[a]

Country	% of total employment
Austria	71.9
Belgium	69.5
Denmark	72.6
Finland	64.5
France	66.6
Germany	64.8
Greece	86.6
Ireland	69.8
Italy	83.5
Luxembourg	73.3
Netherlands	65.2
Portugal	78.9
Spain	81.7
Sweden	68.0
United Kingdom	59.2
Europe-15	**69.7**
Iceland	55.2
Norway	73.8
Switzerland (inc. Liechtenstein)	67.2
Europe-19	**69.7**

Source: European Commission (2004: 78). Estimated by EIM Business & Policy Research; estimates based on Eurostat's Structural Business Statistics and Eurostat's SME Database; also based on *European Economy*, Supplement A, May 2003, and *OECD: Economic Outlook*, no. 71, June 2003; due to rounding, totals may differ slightly from constituting parts.

Note: [a] SMEs are defined here as having 0 to 249 employees.

Table 2.5 The role of SMEs by industrial sector, Europe-19, 2003

Sector	Size category dominance[a]
Extraction (inc. energy)	Large enterprises
Manufacturing	SMEs
Construction	Micro enterprises
Wholesale trade	Micro enterprises
Retail distribution	Micro enterprises
Transport, communication	Large enterprises
Producer services	Large enterprises
Personal services	Micro enterprises
Non-primary private enterprise	Micro enterprises

Source: Derived from European Commission (2004: 30). Estimated by EIM Business & Policy Research; based on Eurostat's Structural Business Statistics and Eurostat's SME Database; also based on *European Economy*, Supplement A, May 2003, and *OECD: Economic Outlook*, no. 71, June 2003.

Note: [a] An industry is 'dominated' by micro enterprises, SMEs or large enterprises if this size category accounts for the largest share of employment.

(over 99 per cent) of the total number of businesses in the SME category, they diverge when it comes to the proportion of *employment* in SMEs. While the Japanese figure (67 per cent) is broadly similar to that for Europe-19, the US proportion is only 49 per cent. This lower figure may be a reflection of the much greater relative importance of one-person businesses in US industry.

There is of course no reason why the SME shares should be uniform across countries. Differences in factor costs, technology, the structure of demand, the maturity of the economy and of particular industries, and the policy environment will all affect the cross-country variation in SME shares.

Variations across markets in the importance of small firms

A key influence on the relative importance of small firms in market terms is likely to be the share of the market required to achieve a minimum efficient scale (MES) of operation (see the end of this chapter for a technical treatment of MES). For a market of a given size, the MES will tend to be larger where substantial capital investment is required before production can occur. This investment may arise because of the nature of the technology or because of the degree to which production is vertically integrated. Similar arguments apply where there is lumpy advertising and promotional expenditure.

Another influence is the market's maturity. In a young industry, which is still establishing itself, and where product development is rapid, there may be more scope for small firms with their typically greater flexibility. Such industries tend to be characterised by fast growth. As a result, existing firms will feel less threatened by new, small entrants; indeed they may be unable themselves to respond to all the opportunities that exist for expansion. At the same time, the smaller firm may not have the financial resources needed to withstand the younger market's greater volatility.

The nature of the product will also affect the share of small firms. For example, where a highly personalised service is required, the small, owner-managed firm often has a distinct advantage. This argument does of course depend on the proposition that such service is not possible, or can be achieved only at higher cost, in larger organisations. Where there is a heavy reliance on advertising to promote products, it might be expected that the smaller firm will be at a disadvantage, since the advertising cost per unit sold will tend to be higher.

In an early study, White (1982) explored some of these issues, looking at the determinants of the share of small firms, measured in sales terms, across US manufacturing industries in 1972. He found significant small firm-share elasticities,[7] with the expected signs, with respect to both the capital:labour ratio (a proxy for capital requirements) and growth (−1.24 and 0.59 respectively). Interestingly, he found that advertising intensity was not significant; indeed, in two of the three equations he estimated, it had a positive sign. White's (1982) study used a small–large dividing line of $5 million in 1972 prices – around $24 million in 2006 prices – although he does report that the results were not especially sensitive to the precise cut-off chosen.

The advertising result is interesting. It may be that the variable is picking up the level of diversification in the industry and the ability of firms of different sizes, selling differentiated products, to coexist. Again, small firms may sometimes be beneficiaries of (rather than losers from) the advertising expenditure of the larger firms, especially if this expenditure leads to the overall growth of the market. It should also be remembered that advertising may *assist* new entry, by bringing products of entrants to the attention of customers.

White (1982) focused exclusively on the United States. His results may not of course hold for other countries, where factor prices and technologies differ. It should also be noted that a substantial proportion of the variation in the small firm share remains unexplained by the factors he considered.

Variations over time

The data presented so far in this section give no indication of how the share of different size bands has behaved *over time*. Chapter 7 provides some summary evidence on what has been happening to the employment share of small firms in the United States and Europe as a whole in recent years. Experience has however differed significantly across countries, a pattern also reflected in data on the proportion of the workforce who are self-employed (Acs et al. 1994). Data for the period 1972–96, shows that in some Organization for Economic Cooperation and Development (OECD) countries this proportion has shown a rising trend, whereas in others it has been falling or remained static (Parker and Robson 2004). See Le (1999) for supporting evidence.

Changes over time in the overall share of small firms raises the question of how far they are due to changes in industrial structure that have led to industries with a bigger (smaller) small firm share becoming relatively more (less) important, and how far to small firms becoming relatively more (less) important in individual industries.

Brock and Evans (1986: 15–22) examined this issue. As in the White (1982) study it is US industry that is analysed. (No similar work has been done for other countries.) Brock and Evans (1986) sought to decompose the change in the relative importance of small firms – in the economy as a whole,[8] and not just manufacturing – over the period 1958 to 1977, a period in which the share of small firms declined, into two components. The first component is the change due to shifts in industrial composition (the industrial composition component: ICC). As data presented earlier in this chapter show, industries differ in the share of activity accounted for by small firms. Thus as industrial composition changes, so the *overall* importance of small firms is likely to change. The second component is the change resulting from increases or decreases in the SME share in individual industries (the small firm share component: SFSC).

ICC may be obtained by calculating what would have happened to the overall share if the share of small firms *in each industry* had remained constant throughout the period; SFSC may be obtained by calculating what would have happened to the overall share accounted for by small firms if industrial structure had remained the same throughout the period.

The Brock and Evans (1986) data may be used to illustrate this decomposition. The overall share of employment in small firms fell by six percentage points from 55 per cent to 49 per cent between 1958 and 1977 (Brock and Evans 1986: 17). If the relative importance of small businesses in each individual industry had remained constant over the period, the overall share of small firms in the economy would have risen from 55 per cent to 59 per cent. Thus the ICC was four percentage points (59 minus 55). If on the other hand the industrial structure had remained the same over the period, the overall share of small firms would have gone down from 55 per cent to 46 per cent. The SFSC was therefore minus nine percentage points (46 minus 55).

The implication of these figures is that while the employment share of small firms in individual industries on average declined over the period, this decline was ameliorated by a shift in industrial structure towards industries which are relatively more conducive to small-scale industries. A broadly similar picture emerges when value added rather than employment is used as the measure. Interestingly however, sales (unlike employment or value added) data show a *negative* ICC which is further magnified by a negative SFSC. One possible explanation for this finding on sales (provided by Lawrence White 1981, quoted in Brock and Evans 1986: 21) is that relatively greater vertical disintegration and a relatively greater rise in capital intensity meant that manufacturing could have a greater sales value with a lower level of employment and value added.

Acs et al. (1999: 9) have shown that overall, the SFSC continued to be negative in the United States in the period 1982–92. This was a decade in which the share of small business (undefined) in private gross income was fairly stable at around 51–2 per cent (Joel Popkin and Company 1997, quoted in Acs et al. 1999: 9), although trends in this share varied across sectors. Kwoka and White (2001) taking a somewhat later period – 1988 to 1996 – in which the employment shares of firms of 100 or fewer employees and 500 or fewer employees both declined – show that for their period, the SFSC was negative.

There are a number of features of the methodology and results of the type of study undertaken by White (1982) and Brock and Evans (1986) that should be noted. First, it is in essence an accounting type of exercise, rather than one that seeks to *explain* trends. Second, the ICC and the SFSC are not independent. For example a shift to smaller scale activity in an industry may make that industry relatively more attractive to consumers, and thus generate growth overall. Despite these limitations, the approach is a useful first step in analysing trends in small business shares. It also serves as a warning that the explanations behind these trends are complex.

Institutions versus owners

So far the focus has been on firms, i.e. economic *institutions*. The corresponding individual that is of interest to us is the small firm *owner*. Such owners may not however be the founders of a business; they may simply have bought an existing, going concern. Owners may thus set up in business in one of two main ways: through the *formation* of a firm, i.e. the setting up of new productive capacity *ab initio*, or through *purchase*. Research on a sample of businesses registering for Value Added Tax (VAT) in the North of England (Johnson and Conway 1997) showed that about 73 per cent were 'formation entrants', although this percentage varied across industrial sectors (the highest percentages of 'purchase entrants' were in retailing and other services).

The distinction between 'formation entry' and 'purchase entry' has not been extensively explored in the literature, although it raises some interesting economic issues about the relative costs of the two different mechanisms, and the reasons why different mechanisms are used in different circumstances. An entirely new operation involves all the costs of putting together the necessary inputs, and establishing both productive activity and a customer base. On the plus side, it also means that the owner is not impeded by established custom and practice. Purchase of an existing business provides the new owner with ready-made productive capacity, and provided buyer loyalty attaches to the business rather than to the previous owner, a customer base. In some cases, e.g. retailing, planning restrictions may mean that the only way to secure a particular location is to buy a business. Of course, if the market is working competitively, the price of an existing business will reflect the relative advantage or disadvantage of purchase over setting up a similar business from scratch.

The two mechanisms also carry implications for the structure of industry. Formation entry initially raises the number of firms, although the knock-on effects of entry on both existing firms and potential entrants will influence the ultimate *net* change in the number of firms. Purchase entry does not, in the first instance, change the number of firms, although again there may be subsequent knock-on effects.

The process of setting up in business is considered further in Chapter 4. It is sufficient to stress here that not all existing small firms will be owned by their founders; and that 'setting up in business' is not synonymous with 'founding a business'. It should also be recognised that many firms are owned by more than one person. Indeed the firm's performance may be affected by how many owners it has.

A key tool of analysis

The long run average cost function: the concept

A variety of analytical tools and concepts has been used in the economic treatment of small firms. It is not possible to consider all of them here. However there is one concept that underpins a good deal of the discussion in this book and it is therefore briefly treated here. That concept is the long run average cost (LRAC) function of the firm. The LRAC function tracks the minimum unit cost of production that can be achieved for different levels of output, when at each level, the firm is producing in the most efficient way, given the technology available, and when it is buying all its inputs at the lowest possible cost. In other words, it is not possible to produce output more cheaply. The term 'long run' is defined conceptually as that period in which the firm is able to make all necessary adjustments to its inputs and production methods. (By contrast, in the 'short run', the firm is often heavily constrained by what it can do, for example, by existing contracts with its suppliers and agreements with its labour force.)

An example of the function, expressed in graphical terms, is given in Figure 2.1. The LRAC curve is drawn for a given technology. An improvement in production technology would shift the curve downwards. This possibility is discussed further below. The curve is sometimes called the 'planning curve', as it traces out the minimum average costs that would be achievable for each level of output, if the production of that output was being planned from scratch.

In the particular example given in Figure 2.1, LRAC falls rapidly, to start with, as the cost of many 'lumpy' items is spread progressively more thinly over bigger output. Examples of such items might be: the salary of the managing director where only one such post is required, whatever the scale of output;[9] central services; certain types of equipment; and research and development costs. LRAC illustrated in Figure 2.1 is minimised at around 20,000 units. This output level may be defined as the 'minimum efficient scale (MES)'. Before this point the firm is obtaining the advantages of 'economies of scale'. After MES, 'diseconomies of scale' set in and LRAC start to rise. There has been a long debate in the literature over why unit costs might rise in this way. One frequently suggested explanation is that the management becomes progressively more complex as the scale of operations expands and as a result, inefficiencies start to build up.

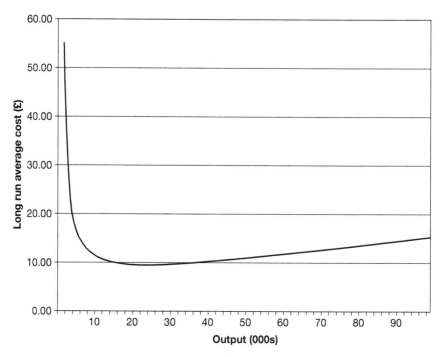

Figure 2.1 Long run average cost and output

The long run average cost function: some issues

It is important to note the following about Figure 2.1. First, it provides only an *illustration* of a possible LRAC cost curve. The position and shape of the curve is likely to vary across sectors. In some sectors the MES may not be achieved until relatively high levels of output; in others it may be reached at relatively low levels of output. Where MES is located is of considerable importance to small firms as Chapter 6 makes clear. For example, there is little point in seeking to set up a small business where MES is at a very high level of output, unless substantial expansion is anticipated. However for any given MES, the *shape* of the LRAC curve may vary. In some cases it may be saucer shaped, so that the cost penalty of working below or above MES may be small; in others it may be more or less V-shaped, with the costs of working at a non-optimal scale – either side of MES – being significantly higher. Some LRAC curves may have significant portions which are relatively flat, i.e. firms of different sizes can operate equally efficiently. The shape of the LRAC curve also has implications for small firms' operations as it will provide a measure of the disadvantage (if any) that such firms may face when competing with larger businesses.

Second, while the assumption of constant technology underpinning Figure 2.1 is a helpful simplifying device, it is far removed from the realities of business life in which learning to do things more efficiently and the development of new and improved products and processes are the stuff of competitive advantage. A key question here is the relationship between size (measured in terms of the firm's output) and the changes in technology the firm generates or adopts. Are larger firms more or less good than their smaller counterparts at developing innovation? In terms of Figure 2.1, there could potentially be a conflict between the *position* of the firm on the curve at any given time and the extent to which it is able to *shift* the curve downwards over time. As Chapter 7 shows there is plenty of evidence to suggest that in some sectors, small firms are an important source of innovation.

Third, the LRAC curve does not necessarily offer any guide as to the level of output that the firm will produce. Profit maximising firms will need to take into account demand conditions as well as costs when coming to their decisions on what output to produce. MES may not represent the profit maximising level of output. However in a highly competitive market, it is likely that the firm will be *forced* to produce near to the MES; otherwise a competitor would be able to produce more cheaply. However in a market where the small firm has some market power, i.e. it is able to protect itself from the competition – for example, by establishing a niche market for itself or by generating a strong reputation – it may find it more profitable to produce below or above MES.

Finally, it needs to be remembered that firms may not *know* what their LRAC are likely to be. The only sure way they may be able to find out is by experimenting with different output levels and then assessing how unit costs change.

Concluding comment

This chapter has considered some of the main reasons why the study of small firms is important, and has looked at some definitional issues and at a key analytical tool in cost analysis. It has also provided some summary data on the importance of small firms in Europe and elsewhere and has explored some explanations behind the trends.

Small firm activity is often seen as the primary expression of entrepreneurship. It is this latter concept that is considered in greater depth in Chapter 3. As this chapter shows, the way in which economists have analysed entrepreneurship has important implications for small firms research.

3 The entrepreneurial function

Introduction

Researchers in the small business field make frequent use of the term 'entrepreneur' to describe a founder or owner of a small business. For example, in Dawson (1996), an edited volume of papers on small firms and regional development, a sixteen-page editorial introduction uses 'entrepreneur,' 'entrepreneurial' or 'entrepreneurship' in this way thirty-five times. Many of the contributors to that volume make similar use of these terms. This kind of usage is widely employed elsewhere in the small business literature.[1]

There can of course be no fundamental objection to the practice of linking the entrepreneurial function specifically to the founding or ownership of small business, provided terms are used consistently and clearly.[2] In any event, such usage need not imply that entrepreneurship does not express itself in other contexts. Nevertheless it is argued later in the chapter that too close an association between entrepreneurship and new and small firms may lead to an unhelpfully narrow focus, and may sometimes impede the effective analysis of the activities of small firms.

This issue is further explored below in the context of some of the insights into the nature of entrepreneurship that economists have contributed over the past 260 years or so. This exercise is inevitably selective; by its nature it ignores the wide range of contributions made from other perspectives.[3]

Many of the seminal insights of economists into the nature of entrepreneurship predate the explosion in small business research since the early 1970s.[4] Indeed, for much of the postwar period, the standard theory of the firm had no real need for any kind of distinctive entrepreneurial input.[5] The assumptions of fully informed economic actors (so that for example, no one makes mistakes in the marketplace, and consumers and producers are stripped of one of the key challenges of economic activity, the accurate processing of market signals),[6] and the tendency to focus on equilibria, rather than on the *processes* by which markets *move* from *dis*equilibria to equilibria, provide little need for such an input.

With this background, it is hardly surprising to find that small business researchers have found it difficult, even if they had the inclination, to make much use of standard neoclassical microeconomic theory. However, if one takes a much longer-term perspective on economic literature, it is clear that economists *have* made some very important contributions to conceptual debates on the role of entrepreneurship which deserve wider consideration today.

The rest of this chapter divides into two sections. In the next section, a number of key contributions in the entrepreneurship literature are reviewed. The final section considers some of the implications of these contributions for the analysis of small business.

Some contributions

Not surprisingly, those economists who have looked in some detail at the entrepreneurial role, are far from unanimous in their views on its essential nature. However, it is not difficult to detect some common themes. While it is easy to oversimplify, four main functions may nevertheless be identified: risk bearing; coordination and management; innovation; and market alertness. Classification of the literature in this way carries some obvious dangers. For example, a number of writers straddle more than one perspective, and some of the literature is not easily classified. This messiness is a reflection of the complex and interrelated nature of the processes involved. Another difficulty is that the literature has not developed in a neat linear fashion through time; there is a good deal of chronological overlap. Nevertheless, the four functions mentioned provide a useful framework for reviewing some key contributions.

Risk bearing

It is Cantillon's *Essai sur la nature du commerce en général* – written around 1730, but not published until 1755 (English translation: Cantillon 1931) – which is the starting point for modern economic analyses of the entrepreneurial function.[7] Cantillon's novel contribution, which has extensive echoes in the writings of others, was to see the entrepreneur as a risk-taker, someone who buys at a certain price, and resells at an uncertain price (1931: 51). The entrepreneur's income is thus a residual – an 'unfixed' wage (1931: 55) – received only after all contractual payments have been met.[8]

For the purposes of this chapter, two elements of Cantillon's approach should be briefly noted. First, he made a clear distinction between the role of the *entrepreneur* as risk-taker, and the role of the *capitalist* as the provider of finance. Entrepreneurs do not have to possess finance for their ventures: even beggars and robbers can qualify (1931: 55). Such a distinction does of course raise the question of what it is the entrepreneur is risking, if it is not his own finance. As Hébert and Link (1982: 19) point out, Cantillon did not directly address this issue, but his *Essai* points to an answer: having grouped together all those who are 'hired people', whose wages are agreed, Cantillon labels the rest entrepreneurs,[9] 'whether they set up with a capital to conduct their enterprise, or are [Entrepreneurs] *of their own labour* without capital, and they may be regarded as living at uncertainty' (Cantillon 1931: 55, italics added). Thus, entrepreneurs who have no capital, nevertheless incur (in modern parlance) the opportunity costs arising from the use of their labour in risk-taking. Entrepreneurs could have used their labour in some other way, perhaps in a 'safe' occupation yielding a contractual income. It may also be the case that when entrepreneurs borrow, they are taking the risk that, should they fail, they will have to employ their labour in paying off their debts.[10]

The second point to note about Cantillon's approach is that he emphasised the entrepreneurial *function*, rather than the individual carrying out the function. People who take risks might also do other things. As demonstrated below, a number of subsequent writers have made a similar point.

Cantillon's basic ideas were developed in a number of directions. For example, in the mid-nineteenth century, the German writer, Heinrich von Thünen (English translation: von Thünen 1960), distinguished clearly between the entrepreneurial gain that derives from the fact that not all risks can be insured, and the yield on the capital invested (1960: 249). He also argued that the residual income received by entrepreneurs as a result of their risk-taking is *not* simply a windfall gain. In times of economic difficulty, entrepreneurs, unlike the paid manager who 'sleeps soundly' after a good day's work (1960: 248), endure sleepless nights working out how they can avoid misfortune. They thus receive 'compensation for [their] industry'. There are costs of being an entrepreneur.

Some seventy years later, Frank Knight (1921) provided a detailed analysis of the nature of the uncertainty borne by entrepreneurs. He distinguished between risk – what he called 'measurable uncertainty' (1921: 233) – and 'unmeasurable uncertainty', which he then collapses to 'uncertainty'. In the case of risk,

> the distribution of the outcome in a group of instances is known (either through calculation *a priori* or from statistics of past experience), while in the case of uncertainty, this is not true, the reason being in general that it is impossible to form a group of instances, because the situation dealt with is in a high degree unique.
>
> (Knight 1921: 233)

For Knight, it is the entrepreneur who specialises in uncertainty bearing. Key sources of the uncertainty the entrepreneur faces lie in the estimation of the scale and nature of future likely demand, and the productivity of the resources employed. If the entrepreneur is successful, he receives a residual – pure profit (Knight 1921: 303f) – of the kind first identified by Cantillon, and made up of the difference between what he receives from the sale of their output and the contractual payments agreed with factors of production. The successful entrepreneur pays less for these factors than what they do in fact prove to be worth. Pure profit is to be distinguished from the competitive return on investment and from wages. Some part of the returns received by the entrepreneur may in fact be a reward for routine management and a return for providing capital.

Since pure profit is a residual, which arises from 'a unique uncertainty resulting from an exercise of ultimate responsibility which in its very nature cannot be insured nor capitalized nor salaried' (Knight 1921: 311), it is fundamentally different from the returns imputed to factors of production via the competitive process.

It is important to note that Knight accepted that the entrepreneurial function might be shared with others, a possibility that is reflected in the research that has been done on entrepreneurial *teams* (see the references quoted in Ucbasaran et al. 2001). For example, some employees may have a profit interest in the business, thus sharing the business uncertainty. Indeed Knight (1921: 300) goes further, arguing that only rarely can an entrepreneur's guarantee of a contractual payment be absolute. There is always *some* uncertainty attached to such a guarantee. This notion of 'diffused entrepreneurship' in an organisation is a powerful insight which has been largely ignored in analyses of Knight's contribution to the literature.

Knight (1921: 300) also reinforced Cantillon's notion that the same person may perform both the entrepreneurial function and other functions. Total specialisation in entrepreneurship alone is very rare.

Coordination and management

It is with the name of J.B. Say that the first serious treatment of the entrepreneur as coordinator is associated.[11] His *Treatise on Political Economy*, first printed in Paris in 1803 (new American edition: Say 1880), sets out the entrepreneurial function. At any given time, Say's entrepreneur

> must employ a great number of hands; at another, buy or order the raw material, collect labourers, find consumers, and give at all times a rigid attention to order and economy; *in a word he must possess the art of superintendence and administration.*
>
> (Say 1880: 330–1, italics added)

To perform this role, the entrepreneur is

> the link of communication, as well between the various classes of producers, one with another, as between the producer and consumer. He directs the business of production, and is the centre of many bearings and relations; he profits by the knowledge and by the ignorance of other people, and by every accidental advantage of production.
>
> (Say 1880: 332)

In Koolman's (1971) words, Say's entrepreneur is 'the linchpin holding together landlord and capitalist, technician and labourer, producer and consumer'. However there is much more to the task than the kind of routine coordination that is implied in the conventional theory of the firm. Demand has to be estimated and likely costs and revenues have to be compared. In all this 'there are abundance of obstacles to be surmounted, of anxieties to be repressed, of misfortunes to be repaired, and of expedients to be devised' (Say 1880: 331). These activities are the stuff of risk bearing, although Say, himself a businessman, preferred to look at them from a coordination perspective, since it is primarily in coordination problems that risk manifests itself in operational terms.

Say's entrepreneur – like Cantillon's, von Thünen's and Knight's – is to be distinguished from that of the capitalist whose function is to provide finance. However in practice, the two roles are frequently combined, and if entrepreneurs have no funds of their own, they must have the ability to attract them from elsewhere.

Alfred Marshall's view of 'business men' as he calls them (1920: 244) – has many similarities with that of Say. Coordination and management play a central role: '[business men] bring together the capital and labour required for the work; they arrange or "engineer" its general plan and superintend its minor details' (Marshall 1920: 244). Marshall, like Say, was however careful to stress the comprehensive, multifaceted nature of the skills that such people need when producing for the general market (as opposed to production for specific orders). In performing this function, Marshall's manufacturer

> must in his first rôle as merchant and organiser of production, have a thorough knowledge of *things* in his own trade. He must have the power of forecasting the broad movements of production and consumption, of seeing where there is an opportunity for supplying a new commodity that will meet a real want or improving the plan of producing an old commodity. He must be able to judge cautiously and undertake risks boldly; and he must of course understand the materials and machinery used in his trade.
> But secondly in this rôle of employer he must be a natural leader of *men*.
> (Marshall 1920: 248; Marshall's italics)

Knowledge, alertness to market opportunities, innovation, judgement, risk taking and leadership are all part and parcel of the business person's functions, although none is developed by Marshall in a distinctive way.

In Marshall's (1920: 252) scheme of things, many of the business person's functions could be carried out by salaried managers, who do not provide any capital. In this sense there may once again be some separation between the entrepreneur and the capitalist. However, Marshall is also clear that the ultimate risk-takers are the shareholders, i.e. the owners of the company.

Innovation

A number of the writers considered so far allude, directly or indirectly, to some form of innovative role for the entrepreneur. However, it was Joseph Schumpeter who identified the entrepreneurial function most closely with innovation. In his

Theory of Economic Development, first published in German in 1911 (English translation: Schumpeter 1934), he defined the function of entrepreneurs as the carrying out of new combinations (1934: 74). Such combinations may be of five different forms: the introduction of a new good, or of a quality of a new good; the introduction of a new production technology; the opening of a new market; the capture of a new source of supply; and the carrying out of the new organisation of any industry (Schumpeter 1934: 66).

It is important to keep Schumpeter's wide-ranging notion of innovation firmly in view. Innovation is not necessarily technological in nature: the development of a new geographical market for an existing product qualifies as an innovation just as much as the introduction of a new method of production or a new product. This catholic view of the nature of innovation is especially helpful in highlighting the many different ways in which markets and products develop. Such activity lies at the centre of the process of 'creative destruction' (Schumpeter 1952: ch. VII), whereby the old is continually being destroyed by the new. Innovation is the vehicle by which established equilibria are destroyed.

There are several features of Schumpeter's approach which are relevant here. First, Schumpeter (1934: 75), like many previous writers on the entrepreneur, made a clear conceptual distinction between the entrepreneurial and capitalist functions, even though he fully acknowledged that the same person often exercised both. Risk bearing however is no part of the Schumpeterian entrepreneurial function (1934: 75, 137).[12] Second, his entrepreneurs might be salaried employees, provided they are engaged in carrying out new combinations. Third, individuals are acting as Schumpeterian entrepreneurs only *while they are innovating*:

> it is just as rare for anyone always to remain an entrepreneur throughout the decades of his active life as it is for a businessman never to have a moment in which he is an entrepreneur, to however modest a degree.
>
> (Schumpeter 1934: 78)

Entrepreneurship is not a lasting condition; at the same time, most business people will exercise such a role at some time or other. It is also interesting that Schumpeter implies that entrepreneurial activity may vary along some scale of importance.

Finally, it appears that Schumpeter linked the entrepreneurial function with formation:

> new combinations are, as a rule, embodied, as it were, in new firms which do not arise out of the old ones but start producing beside them; . . . in general it is not the owner of the stage coaches who builds railways.
>
> (Schumpeter 1934: 66)

It is unclear however whether Schumpeter's 'new firm' includes what today would be called a cross-entrant – an existing firm operating elsewhere, but new to the industry in question – but the basic point that established operators may not be able, or wish to perceive new developments, remains. This point is clearly significant for the current analysis of small business.

Market alertness

Perhaps the most recent substantive contribution to the analysis of the entrepreneurial function has come from the work of Kirzner (1973, 1979, 1985, 1997). Developing ideas from Mises and Hayek, Kirzner sees the entrepreneurial element in decision making as 'alertness to possibly new worthwhile goals and to possibly newly available resources' (Kirzner 1973: 35), a phase which is reminiscent of Marshall (see above).

Kirzner (1973: 39) argues that such alertness 'to hitherto unnoticed opportunities' is essential to the proper understanding of market processes. The *pure* entrepreneur owns no resources, and owners of firms are entrepreneurs only in so far as they exercise alertness. Thus ownership and entrepreneurship are two separate functions. The crucial question for deciding who is exercising the latter function in the firm concerns 'whose vision and alertness to hitherto unnoticed opportunities is responsible for the effective decisions of the . . . firm' (Kirzner 1973: 57). It is by this exercise of alertness – the process of *discovery* – that markets move towards equilibria.

The function of Kirzner's entrepreneur may be illustrated by a straightforward example of arbitrage (1985: 158–9). Kirzner uses the example of a good being bought and sold in two adjacent rooms. The buyers and sellers in each room are unaware of the presence of their counterparts in the other room. In one room, the price of the good has settled at a low price, and in the other, the prevailing price is high. Kirzner's entrepreneur discovers the opportunity – which had always been there, but no one had previously realised it – for buying at a lower price in the first room and then selling at a higher price in the second.

The arbitrage function may not only be exercised in terms of product markets. It clearly has applications where a factor *and* a product market are involved. Entrepreneurs may seek to buy in factor services at a price which they perceive to be lower than the value that they can realise for them in the product market. Arbitrage may also involve the production of new or improved goods and services.

Kirznerian market alertness is exercised in the expectation of entrepreneurial profits. Such profits may in the event turn out to be negative, but *ex ante*, of course, the entrepreneur envisages only positive returns. Kirzner is clear that entrepreneurship is costless: 'alertness is not something about which a decision can be made *not* to deploy it' (1985: 24; Kirzner's italics). In this sense, it has no opportunity cost, and any pure profit that results cannot be seen as a factor return in the conventional sense. It is not therefore meaningful to talk of the marginal product of the entrepreneurial factor, or of its supply curve. At the same time, it does make sense, even for Kirzner (see for example Kirzner 1973:

242) to examine the degree to which the external environment is more or less encouraging to the exercise of alertness.

Kirzner's view does, of course, have much in common with that of Schumpeter. However, his emphasis is different. While Schumpeter is concerned with the *introduction* of innovation (in its broadest sense), Kirzner is preoccupied with the ability to *see* where the new opportunities lie:

> Entrepreneurship . . . is not so much the introduction of new products or of new techniques of production as the ability to *see* where new products have become unsuspectedly valuable to consumers and where new methods of production have, unknown to others, become feasible . . . the function of the entrepreneur consists not of *shifting* the curves of costs or of revenues which face him, but *of noticing that they have in fact shifted*.
>
> (Kirzner 1973: 81; Kirzner's italics)

It is also the case, as Casson (2003: 230) has pointed out, that while Kirzner is primarily concerned with how entrepreneurs operate within a given set of markets – though not within a *given* set of ends and objectives – Schumpeter's entrepreneurs actually *create and destroy* markets.

Kirzner's process of market discovery has much in common with Shane and Venkataraman's (2000) concept of entrepreneurship, although these authors are concerned not only with discovery, but also with the evaluation and exploitation of new opportunities.

The Kirznerian description of entrepreneurial activity has attracted considerable debate (see for example Hébert and Link 1982: 96f; Schultz 1990: 35f). Schultz's approach is particularly worth noting. His analysis of the entrepreneur has a good deal in common with that of Kirzner, but he takes a much more conventional, down-to-earth, view of the entrepreneur as the agent of resource reallocation in the economy. To Schultz (1990: 20), the notion that the entrepreneur is somehow more 'alert' than others is to romanticise the entrepreneurial function. The entrepreneur is simply responding to disequilibrium in his own particular sphere by reallocating resources. This kind of activity is not restricted to business people, but extends to such people as housewives and students at different times in their lives (for Schultz, there is no separate class of entrepreneurs).

Furthermore, according to Schultz, entrepreneurial ability can be enhanced by experience, education and health. He points, for example, to the evidence from agriculture that education increases the allocative, i.e. entrepreneurial, abilities of farmers (Schultz 1990: 92). In this sense entrepreneurial ability may be seen as a form of human capital. The function of reallocation takes time and there is consequently an opportunity cost to the exercise of entrepreneurship. In Schultz's view therefore there is no reason why entrepreneurship should not be analysed in conventional factor supply and demand terms.

Some implications

The previous section provided a whistle-stop tour of seminal contributions to the debate over the essential nature of entrepreneurship and has given a flavour of the issues involved. Four 'core' substantive functions were identified. Each of these functions has an important contribution to make in the successful pursuit of business, although each is likely to vary in significance, depending on the particular challenges and opportunities that a firm faces and on its stage of development. Some of the implications of this literature for the analysis of small business activity are now explored.

The wider context

The kinds of functions described in the contributions reviewed here are performed in all sorts of businesses: large and small; young and old. A key question therefore concerns the way in which different business environments and circumstances might generate differences in the optimal mix of businesses. In some contexts, the best vehicle for pursuing (say) innovation may be the large, established firm; in others it may be the new, small firm.[13] Acs and Audretsch (1990), for example, have provided some useful insights into when small firms are likely to be most appropriate for innovation. Again, in industries where the production function is characterised by economies of scale, coordination may be most efficiently conducted in the larger unit; in some personal services, the opposite may be true. There may be some cases where a *mix* of firm sizes and/or ages is most appropriate. Penrose's (1980: 222–5) notion of 'interstices' helps to illustrate this point, with small firms in some cases finding their niches 'between' the large firms.

There may also be important country differences in the regulatory regime and in culture that influence the optimal scale of new and small firm activity (Davidsson and Wiklund 2001).

The above suggests that in any analysis of the contribution of small firms, it is important to consider the *appropriateness* of small scale in different contexts, and the *interrelationships* between different sizes of firm. Similarly, the role of new firms can be fully assessed only in the context of the contribution of firms of other generations and the interrelationships between them. There is thus a good case for putting any discussion of small firms into the larger context of the implications and effects of *scale* and *age*, which implies looking at *all* sizes and ages rather than restricting consideration to (say) micro enterprise or new formations.

A further widening of the context for analysing small business derives from the particular contribution of Schultz (1990), who argues that the reallocating activity of entrepreneurs is to be found in all walks of life. This in turn poses the question of how far the dividing line between for-profit and not-for-profit – itself a rather blurred distinction – is a useful one when it comes to entrepreneurial activity. As incomes grow, and leisure activities increase, the study of the mechanisms for progress in non- commercial ventures such as clubs, charities, universities and other not-for-profit organisations, is likely to take on increasing importance.[14] This book focuses exclusively on the commercial sector, but the wider relevance of the entrepreneurship literature for not-for-profits should be recognised, especially given the growth in private–public partnerships in recent years. It would be very surprising indeed if current research knowledge of small firms in the commercial sector were irrelevant to the analysis of not-for-profit activities.

The emphasis on functions

The contributions outlined in this chapter have emphasised *functions*, rather than individuals – Alfred Marshall, of all the writers, best captures this aspect – who may move in and out of entrepreneurial-type activities over time, and who may share such activities with others. Little is known however about why and how this movement and sharing occurs, although the current interest in team work has already been indicated.

Knight (1921) raises some interesting issues for the analysis of small firms when he discusses the sharing of the uncertainty bearing function. Knight's point is that it is rarely possible to provide an absolutely cast-iron guarantee of a contractual payment. In other words, the distinction between contractual and residual payments is not completely clear cut. This in turn may mean that the employees taken on by a small firm owner may also be bearing some of the uncertainty associated with the business. Employers and employees are in it together. A fair amount is already known about employment in small firms – see Chapter 7 – but relatively little research has been done on why some individuals are attracted into smaller firms *as employees*, or on the distribution of the risk across employees and the owner.

Another implication of the emphasis on functions is that it raises the question of *the relationship between* the entrepreneurial function and other functions. It would be helpful to know something about the relative importance (for business success) of different functions in different contexts, how they interact, and the degree to which these functions act as substitutes or complements, since small business owners and founders will vary considerably in the bundle of skills and attributes that they bring to their tasks. The interrelationship between entrepreneurship and the provision of capital – a link made by a number of writers – is likely to be particularly important.

The literature is also valuable in emphasising functions that have been less widely studied than others. In particular there is relatively little literature on the factors that influence Kirzner-type market alertness. Why do some people spot opportunities when others do not? How might alertness be encouraged? How do entrepreneurs learn from their market participation?

The ' intensity' of entrepreneurship

The discussion on the functional aspects of entrepreneurship serves to highlight an important aspect of entrepreneurial activity: it is likely to vary in its intensity across time and situations. For example some innovations are less (more) 'innovative' in some sense than others; some entrepreneurial initiatives are less (more) risky than others; and so on. To equate (say) all innovation or risk-taking as equivalent in some sense is unlikely to be helpful either in terms of the analysis of the factors that influence such activity or in terms of policy formulation. If such differences are to be allowed for in any consistent way it would be necessary to establish some appropriate metric, a formidable challenge. A first step might however be some form of subjective ranking by 'experts'.

The failure to recognise differences in the intensity of entrepreneurial activity is often expressed in the preoccupation in policy discussions with 'high level' entrepreneurship, usually involving major innovative developments in high tech industries and in the lack of interest in more mundane, 'low level' entrepreneurial activity, which often takes place in well-established service industries. In overall quantitative terms, the latter may arguably have a greater impact.

The supply of entrepreneurship

It is clear from the previous section that there is considerable debate over the appropriateness of analysing entrepreneurship in terms of its 'costs' or 'supply'. It is not however necessary to take a stance on this debate to argue that different environments are likely to generate different levels of entrepreneurial activity. There is now a very substantial literature on the factors which determine variations in business formation and self-employment activity across space, time and industry (see Chapter 5), but much less is known about the most congenial environment for encouraging entrepreneurship in the wider senses examined here. Too close a focus on new and small firms may miss some key issues associated with the encouragement of entrepreneurial activity in the economy. It also needs to be recognised that many small firms may display only very limited entrepreneurial activity or potential.

Concluding comment

This chapter has sought to demonstrate that the analysis of small business has much to learn from the economic literature on entrepreneurial activity. This literature raises important questions about the essential nature of such activity, and its relationship with other activities, and about the appropriate framework for analysing small business. The broader perspective that the literature provides needs to be borne in mind throughout the rest of the book.

For the sake of clarity, the terms 'entrepreneur' or 'entrepreneurship' will not be used in the rest of this book, unless the work of others is being quoted or unless the meaning is clear. Such abstinence is also an acknowledgement of the wide range of treatments and definitions that these terms have been given in the literature. However many of the concepts and activities reviewed in this chapter are directly relevant for the analysis of small firms contained elsewhere in this book.

4   Setting up in business

Introduction

As Chapter 7 demonstrates, the small business sector performs an important set of economic functions. It is therefore vital to consider the factors affecting the decision to set up in business, since it is via this process that the small business sector is regenerated. In the next section, a simplified approach to the analysis of the setting up process is presented. Some of the assumptions underlying this approach are then explored. The chapter concludes by examining some of the characteristics of the self-employed, as these characteristics may provide some further clues about what leads individuals into business.

Before proceeding further, it is helpful to make three preliminary points. First, the term 'self-employment' is used here as a shorthand to cover any form of own account activity. The term therefore covers individuals who set up their own company even though they may, for some legal purposes, be regarded as employees of their companies.

Second, it should be noted that setting up in business may not always involve the formation of a firm, though this will usually be the case (see p. 16).

Third, it is important to realise that self-employment activities may be only part-time. For example, someone who sets up in business may continue to work for an employer: the person's business activities may be confined to times which are not in 'working' hours, or the terms of the paid employment contract may enable the person to run both self- and paid employment in parallel. Such a combination of activities is especially likely in the early days of self-employment when the uncertainty surrounding the outcome of the individual's business activities may be particularly high. Even after the business venture has shown some signs of success, individuals may still prefer to employ someone to run the firm for them, rather than to engage in the activity themselves. Such a strategy permits the transfer of some of the risk associated with self-employment to the employee; if the firm fails, it is the employee, not the owner, who loses his or her job.

The decision to set up in business

A simple model

The process leading up to the formation process is likely to be complex and often drawn out. Thinking about and planning a new business venture often takes considerable time and will involve a whole series of decisions on the way. In recent years a number of studies on 'nascent entrepreneurs' – those individuals who are seriously thinking about, or are in the process of establishing a business – has led to a substantially increased knowledge of this gestation activity (see for example Davidsson 2005; Grilo and Thurik 2005; Parker 2005).

If setting up involves a process that takes time, talk of *the* decision to set up is clearly a considerable simplification. However it does enable the identification of the key economic influences at work. The essence of the model presented here is that at any point in time, the individual considering setting up may be seen as implicitly comparing the perceived future income from entry into self-employment, with the perceived future income from the best alternative use of his or her time. Movement into business will occur where the difference between the perceived incomes is greater than the costs of making the transfer. These costs include the initial investment costs, the costs of search, e.g. for premises and customers, the administrative costs, e.g. the legal expenses in setting up in business, and so on.

Assuming that the returns and costs are known with certainty, and that the choice is between future full-time self-employment, yielding a present value (PV) of self-employment income, π^{pv} and future full-time paid employment, yielding a PV of paid employment income, y^{pv}, the individual will move into self-employment where

$$\pi^{pv} - y^{pv} > t \qquad (4.1)$$

where t = the costs of setting up in business which are assumed here (for simplicity's sake) to be a lump sum incurred at the time of entry.

The above is of course highly abstract. The basic approach – often with substantial adaptation – has however been widely used (see for example Creedy and Johnson 1983; Storey and Jones 1987; Robson 1991; Black et al. 1996) in the empirical analysis of formation activity.

A push-pull distinction

One of the implications of the framework outlined here is that a conceptual distinction may be made between 'push' and 'pull' factors at work in the decision to move into business. Individuals may be 'pushed' into self-employment when the left-hand side of Equation (4.1) rises as a result of a decline in y^{pv}. Thus a fall in wages or job prospects, e.g. through actual or threatened redundancy, may induce someone to set up in business. Such a proposition is consistent with the evidence provided by Evans and Leighton (1989) that the likelihood of someone entering self-employment is negatively related to the individual's wage level.

The possible role of unemployment in stimulating movement into business has long been acknowledged in the literature (Schumpeter 1939: 94, fn 3; Oxenfeldt 1943: 120–3; Steindl 1945: 61; Storey 1982: 112). There is also some evidence (see the section 'Who are the self-employed?' below) that suggests that at least for the United States, the probability of having self-employment rather than paid employment status in the labour market is positively related to experience of unemployment. As Chapter 5 shows, the possible role of unemployment as a stimulus for setting up has been widely considered in empirical work on regional differences in formation activity. The results are however mixed.

The 'pull' factor will be at work when the right-hand side of Equation (4.1) rises as a result of π^{pv} increasing. This may happen as a result, for example, of improved macroeconomic conditions. Again, as Chapter 5 shows, numerous empirical studies have endeavoured to capture this effect using a wide variety of measures. Of course what will often happen is that both π^{pv} and y^{pv} move, and often in the same direction. Thus for example, when y^{pv} falls, say as the result of a worsening economic environment, that same environment may also depress π^{pv}. The two returns may not however move to the same extent.

The push-pull distinction outlined above corresponds loosely to the distinction between 'necessity-based' and 'opportunity-based' 'early-stage entrepreneurial activity' made in the *Global Entrepreneurship Monitor (GEM)*: see for example Minniti et al. (2006: 21f).[1] In Chapter 5 a more detailed technical description from *GEM* of what constitutes early-stage entrepreneurial activity and of its prevalence in 2005 in thirty-five countries is considered (see pp. 45–47). Here the focus is on the underlying motivation for engaging in start-up activity.

Necessity-based early-stage entrepreneurial activity was defined by *GEM* as occurring when individuals are pushed into business 'because all other options for work are either absent or unsatisfactory'. Opportunity-based activity however occurs when businesses are started by individuals who 'want to exploit a perceived business opportunity' (Minniti et al. 2006: 21). From its survey work, *GEM* found that for the thirty-five countries analysed, the overwhelming majority of early-stage entrepreneurs in 2005 were opportunity driven: the average for the ratio of opportunity-based to necessity-based activity was almost six. There is however considerable variation in this ratio across countries. High income countries tend for example, to have a higher ratio than middle income countries (7.87 compared with 2.67: see Minniti et al. 2006: 23). It is also worth noting that the *GEM* evidence suggests that opportunity-based early-stage entrepreneurship is less likely to fail. In other words, motivation affects the likelihood of success.

Exploring the assumptions

How certain are the returns?

A number of simplifying assumptions underpin Equation (4.1). Perhaps the key assumption was that the monetary returns from both self-employment and the alternative were known with certainty. This assumption hardly reflects reality. It is more realistic to portray the potential entrant as facing a *distribution* of possible returns of both π^{pv} and y^{pv}. This distribution will embody a subjective assessment by the individual of the probability of different outcomes. How the individual then acts on this perceived distribution will depend on his or her attitude to risk. For example, the person may be concerned only with the expected value of the distribution, i.e. he or she may be indifferent between distributions that have the same expected value, but a different spread. Alternatively, the precise spread of possible outcomes may matter.

It is of course the individual's *perceptions* of possible outcomes that are all important. These perceptions are likely to be affected by a range of factors, including discussions with friends, relatives and advisers, and the individual's own assessment of likely costs and revenues. This in turn will be affected by his or her evaluation of future business conditions.

These perceptions may in the event turn out to be wildly inaccurate. Indeed, it may only be by *actually engaging in business* that more accurate information can be obtained, not only about the market potential of the products or services involved and the business environment, but also about the founder's own skills and abilities. This notion of entrepreneurial learning is considered in the seminal article by Jovanovic (1982). Stam et al. (2005) have pointed out that this learning may not simply be about the initial endowment of entrepreneurial 'talent'. It may also involve *active* learning that enables the founder to perform better as a result of his or her experience. If this active learning takes place it would be expected that there would be some adjustment through time in the perception of the two future income streams.

There is some evidence to suggest that small business entrants typically overestimate their prospects. The high exit rates for small businesses provide some suggestive evidence on this score. For example, Ashworth et al. (1998) report evidence that in the United Kingdom, over 50 per cent of VAT regis- trations deregister within six years, a finding confirmed by more recent government data (www.sbs.gov.uk). The Department of Trade and Industry (DTI 2004a) shows that 57 per cent of *companies* incorporated in 1999 had ceased to be active by March 2004. VAT data for the 1990s suggest that there may have been some improvement in the six year survival rate in the 1990s,[2] but it is still low. There are of course all sorts of limitations with these VAT data (see p. 48). Deregistration may not mean business failure. It may also be that those registering for VAT and/or setting up a company, do so *knowing* that they will be sufficiently successful within a fairly short period to get out of business, i.e. they *may have planned* to stay in business only for a short period

– perhaps for a specific purpose. However it would be surprising if most of the deregistrations were not of businesses which were set up with longer term horizons in view, but which experienced returns that were lower than anticipated.

Some further support for the proposition that small business owners tend to overestimate their prospects comes from the interview study by Ashworth et al. (1998) who compared the employment *estimates* made by a sample of owners of new small businesses for six and twelve months ahead, with the *actual* employment that occurred. Only surviving businesses were included in this exercise. Employment is not entirely satisfactory as measure of business success but it was the best available to the researchers.

Ashworth et al. (1998) showed that the owners modestly but systematically overestimated their employment growth – by about 10 per cent for the six-month forecast, and 20 per cent for the twelve-month forecast. It is possible that this result reflected a bias generated by the interview itself: the interviewees may have thought that a bullish forecast would show them in a good light. However, considerable effort was made to impress on the interviewees that no particular type of response was being sought. Interviewees were also told that the interviewer would be returning to compare actuals against forecast.

A number of interpretations could be placed on the results. It might be, for example, that all the interviewees were affected by a common 'shock' that adversely affected their businesses after they made the forecast. The investigators were unable to identify any such shock. A more plausible explanation is that the owners adopted an optimistic interpretation of market prospects and their own abilities to exploit those opportunities. Such an interpretation is in line with the survey-based finding by Cooper et al. (1988), that US founders tend to show a 'remarkable level of optimism'. Their study of individuals who had recently gone into business found that 81 per cent of their respondents gave odds of success as seven out of ten or higher, much greater than the five out of ten that would be justified by the relevant survival data.

Interestingly, the Ashworth et al. (1998) study suggested that the error may in some way be related to misinterpretation by the owners of the information embodied in the firm's current size, and indeed the rate of change in that size. For example, owners who have seen their businesses grow rapidly in the past may incorrectly assume that the same rate of growth can be sustained into the future. The likelihood of forecast error problems may be accentuated where innovation – with all its uncertainties – and/or an unstable market environment are involved. The study also suggests, not implausibly, that the older the business the lower the error; owners learn about both their business and their own forecasting abilities through time.

A further finding from Ashworth et al. (1998) should be noted: they found that of the twenty-one businesses that exited during the study, and were hence not included in the survey of forecasting accuracy, over 75 per cent were confident at the beginning of the period that they would survive in business.

Full or part-time self-employment?

Equation (4.1) also assumed that the choice facing the individual was either future full-time self-employment or future full-time paid employment. This rather stark either/or choice is the basis on which the setting-up decision is usually modelled in empirical studies. But the real world is more complex. As indicated earlier, the two states may be combined. Again, an anticipated career path may involve a *sequence* of different labour market states. And, as suggested in the previous section, some of the *un*employed may consider setting up. For them, the alternative to a future self-employment income may consist of, or include, unemployment benefit rather than wages. Another complexity arises because some individuals may be 'serial entrepreneurs', i.e. individuals who move from one business venture to another. In the course of their lifetimes, they may set up several businesses in sequence. Figures quoted in Westhead et al. (2005) suggest that perhaps 19–25 per cent of owner managers come into this category. Notwithstanding these complications, Equation (4.1) does nevertheless help to identify the key influences.

Monetary versus non-monetary returns

Empirical work has typically concentrated on monetary returns. But non-monetary factors are likely to figure prominently in many setting up decisions. For example, there is a considerable body of survey evidence (see for example Johnson 1986: 71–2) to suggest that the desire for independence – to be one's own boss – is an important factor driving the set-up decision. Employees may leave a business to work on their own account because they cannot get their ideas, e.g. on potential innovations or on management approaches, accepted. A good example of this kind of spin-off is given by Audretsch (1999: 9–10), who describes the reasons behind the departure of Bob Noyce, the founder of Intel, from his previous employer. This departure came about because this business would not go along with Noyce's vision of a company whose employees were all tied in to the future of the business via stock options, and where hierarchical and bureaucratic management styles (e.g. reserved parking slots; executive dining rooms) were absent.

There is also some evidence (Blanchflower and Oswald 1991) to suggest that some self-employed place greater emphasis on the need for social acceptance;[3] one explanation for this finding is that self-employment may provide one route through which individuals who lack other social 'credentials', e.g. educational qualifications, are able to obtain some form of recognition. On the other hand, paid employment typically offers greater security than self-employment. It is known for example that the spread of self-employment income is greater than that for paid employment (Parker 1999).

It is also worth noting that there may be some non-monetary elements in *t* in Equation (4.1). For example, there may be considerable stress arising from the transfer. The presence of non-monetary considerations may further complicate the analysis of the set-up decision, although there may be grounds for legitimately ignoring them – for example, in cross-section work on industrial variations in formation rates, it may be argued that non- monetary characteristics of both paid and self-employment do not tend to be industry specific (Creedy and Johnson 1983).

Who are the self-employed?

In this section some of the empirical work that has been done on the characteristics of those people who set up in business on an own account basis is examined. This is a vast area and it is necessary to be selective. It should be recognised that studies on this topic relate to particular times or periods, and to a particular environment. For example, the relatively high incidence of self-employment among Ugandan Asians in UK retailing in the mid-1970s reflects the effect of the expulsions made under Idi Amin's regime. Again, the propensity of particular groups to be self-employed may vary depending on what opportunities these groups face for both employment and small business activity. Johnson and Rodger (1983) showed that significant numbers of managers from the divisional headquarters of a multinational company who were affected by the downsizing of their company entered self-employment when they were made redundant. This transition, which in many cases was assisted by the company, would certainly not have occurred if the company had not been forced by market conditions to scale down its operations. Studies of characteristics of the self-employed may also vary across countries. The findings outlined below should be interpreted in this context.

The main concern in this section is with the propensity to have self-employment status in the labour market.[4] At this stage no distinction is made between individuals on the basis of how successful they are. It is important to note this point, as the characteristics of survivors and non-survivors, and those of relatively 'successful' and 'unsuccessful' survivors almost certainly differ. This issue is considered further in Chapter 6.

At the risk of oversimplifying, characteristics may be categorised under three broad headings: personal characteristics and family background; labour market experience; and financial characteristics.

Personal characteristics and family background

Age

A number of investigators have looked at the incidence of self-employment among different age groups. For example, Evans and Leighton (1989) reported in their study of US white males that the self-employment propensity increases at a diminishing rate until about the age of 40, after which it remains fairly level until about 60, when it starts to rise again.[5] Evans and Leighton's results are generally supported by other studies (see the summary in Le 1999).

The rise in the proportion of self-employed with age in the twenties and thirties may reflect a variety of factors, including greater labour market experience, which, inter alia, ensures a higher chance of survival, greater willingness to take risk and, perhaps most importantly, more accumulated capital. As the forties are approached, there may be less willingness to take risk. After 60, self-employment may become popular as a source of supplementary income for individuals who have retired from paid employment. It should be noted that Evans and Leighton (1989) also found that the propensity to *enter* self-employment is relatively stable between the mid-twenties and mid-forties. This finding can be reconciled with the rise in the propensity to be self-employed up to 40 by the fact that survival tends to rise with age.

Education and intelligence

How far education affects the propensity to be self-employed has been widely investigated. The results of these studies have been varied: contrast for example, Evans and Leighton (1989) who show a positive effect of education on self-employment propensity among US white males and Evans (1989) who reports a negative effect among Australian immigrants. The mixed nature of this outcome reflects a number of factors. The a priori arguments do not point unambiguously to a particular result. On the one hand, it may be argued that education increases an individual's ability to manage his or her own business, and hence makes self-employment more attractive; on the other, it is also likely to enhance the opportunities in paid employment. The outcome will depend on the particular context. It should also be noted that the result on education may depend on what other variables are included. For example, Le (1999) has pointed out that in general, studies which do not allow for occupational status, report a positive (or, sometimes, weak negative) effect of education, whereas in studies which do include it, the effect of education is negative.

There is some evidence – from the Netherlands – to suggest that general intelligence, as measured (say) by IQ scores, may be more important in having a positive effect on the propensity to be self-employed than formal education, as measured by test scores (De Wit and Van Winden 1989).[6]

Psychological characteristics

Some economists have included psychological characteristics in their analysis of self-employment propensities. Blanchflower and Oswald (1991) have examined some of these characteristics in their study of the employment status in 1981 of over 12,500 individuals, all of whom were born in March 1958 and who were part of the National Child Development Study (NCDS) in the United Kingdom. They looked at a number of psychological measures based on reports made by teachers when the respondents were 7 years of age. There is some suggestion from these measures that overall, self-employed people were less inclined than average to be unforthcoming as children, and more likely than average to show hostility to other children. These characteristics are however very much less significant in the case of self-employed people who are not in a family firm. At the same time, this group of self-employed have a significant and positive coefficient on the anxiety-for-acceptance score,[7] a finding that is in line with the earlier suggestion that self-employment may be one route through which individuals who lack other expressions of status (e.g. academic qualifications) are able to obtain some form of recognition.

Evans and Leighton (1989) found that individuals with a higher 'internal locus of control', as measured by the appropriate psychological index, known as the Rotter score,[8] were more likely to be self-employed. The argument here is that such individuals are more likely to believe that their performance depends on their own actions. Interestingly, Evans and Leighton found that the coefficient on education becomes insignificant, once allowance is made for this factor. This raises some interesting questions on the relationship between the Rotter score and education. Perhaps those who have a higher internal locus of control are more likely to seek out educational opportunities. Another possibility is that it is in fact education that leads to the higher internal locus of control in the first place.

Considerable care must be exercised in interpreting these psychological insights. However they are at least consistent with the plausible proposition that people who are self-reliant, extrovert, who have some aggressive instinct, and who want their achievements to be recognised by others, are more likely to make it into self-employment.

Ethnicity

Ethnic origin has also been considered. Borjars and Bronars (1989) show that in 1980 in the United States, Whites and Asians had very similar self-employment rates (just under 12 per cent). This is far higher than the rate for Blacks (4.5 per cent) and Hispanics (7 per cent). Jones et al. (1994: 146) quote evidence to show that in the United Kingdom, native whites had a self-employment rate of around 6 per cent in the early 1980s while for Other Europeans, those with an ethnic origin in the Indian subcontinent and those whose ethnic origin was African Caribbean, the percentages were 8.4, 7.9 and 3.1 respectively. A key question here is how far ethnic origin is proxying for other variables. In this context it should be noted that Borjas and Bronars (1989) also show that the variation in self-employment rates across Whites, Blacks and Hispanics cannot be explained by differences in characteristics across these groupings.[9] Rather it may be the incentive to become self-employed that may differ.

Minniti (2006) has provided a fascinating additional piece of evidence on ethnic differences. She shows that although black Americans are relatively poorly represented among the self-employed, they are nearly twice as likely as whites to *try* to set up in business. Furthermore, she shows that this higher propensity to set up is not explained by socio-demographic differences and that black Americans tend to be more optimistic about their prospects when it comes to business and less fearful about failure. The big challenge here of course is *why* black Americans' higher propensity to set up in business is not followed through into the statistics on established businesses. Minniti suggests very plausibly that the answer lies in the constraints faced by black Americans in setting up and then surviving.

Other characteristics

The effects of numerous other personal characteristics on self-employment propensity have been investigated. For example, work has been done on whether married status influences the self-employment propensity. On the one hand it may increase the availability of capital,[10] provide a ready supply of trusted labour, and give background stability for entrepreneurial risk-taking. On the other hand, increased home responsibilities may make an individual more reluctant to launch out on an own-business venture. Most studies suggest a positive relationship (see Le 1999).

As far as family links are concerned, Evans and Leighton (1989) show – in the case of US white males – that where the father is a manager, an individual is more likely to be self-employed, suggesting, not unreasonably, that family experience relevant to self-employment may encourage individuals to set up on their own. De Wit and Van Winden (1989) show an even more direct link in their study of Dutch data: the self-employment propensity is raised where a father has self-employment experience. This is hardly surprising as there are likely to be fewer psychological barriers to setting up where someone already has family experience of self-employment status.

Labour market experience

The evidence suggests that the longer the experience in the labour market, the greater the propensity to be self-employed (see for example Borjas 1986; Evans and Leighton 1989). This result is in line with the results on age, and similar arguments apply. Le (1999) has pointed out that *where* labour market experience is obtained may also be important. For example an immigrant who has gained most of his or her labour market experience abroad will typically be less well placed, in terms of local knowledge, than a national when it comes to setting up in business.

Another finding presented by Evans and Leighton was that the frequency of job change and experience of unemployment enhanced the likelihood of self-employment. The finding on the former is plausible: individuals who are prepared to make job changes, are also likely to be better equipped to make the significant changes required to set up on an own account basis. The finding on the latter must however be seen in the context of the mixed results of studies that have looked at the role of unemployment in stimulating formation activity (see Chapter 5).

Lazear (2002) has looked at the skills mix of those who establish a business, using data on graduates from Stanford. Fascinatingly, he found that founders tended to be more balanced individuals, with an *array* of skills, rather than specialists in a particular area. He argues that his results support a 'jack-of-all-trades' view of entrepreneurs.

Financial characteristics

Blanchflower and Oswald (1991) were able to use a question on inheritance and gifts in the NCDS to explore how far the propensity to be self-employed is affected by the supply of finance. They found that up to £14,000 (around £36,000 in 2006 prices) inheritances and gifts increase the probability that someone will be self-employed, but that beyond this level, the probability declines.[11] The decline in this probability may reflect a number of factors including the fact that there will come a point where an inheritance or gift removes the need to work. Even when Blanchflower and Oswald (1991) allow for the possibility that some individuals may enter self-employment in a family firm which they have inherited, by excluding all those who are self-employed *and* in a family firm, the effects of inheritance or gifts are still positive. Furthermore, the availability of such funds appears to have a disproportionate effect on the probability of being self-employed. Blanchflower and Oswald (1991) estimate that an inheritance of £5000 (about £13,000 in 2006 prices) approximately doubles this probability. The effects of a given value of inheritances and gifts on the self-employment propensity is likely to vary across firm start-up size, with the smaller firms relying more heavily on this source.

Blanchflower and Oswald's (1991) evidence is consistent with the finding by Evans and Leighton (1989) that movement into self-employment is positively related to family net worth. However it should be noted that this finding is also consistent with second generation owners inheriting family firms.

Concluding comment

This chapter has suggested a rather abstract, yet insightful, way of looking at the formation decision from the standpoint of the would-be business person. The abstractions involved are severe, but the approach does serve to highlight the interdependence between the factors affecting paid employment or unemployment and those influencing self-employment. The latter, and conditions surrounding it, cannot be analysed in isolation. Thus, for example, if government policy changes the benefits regime for the unemployed or payroll taxes, an impact on the attractiveness of self-employment would be expected.

It has been demonstrated that the outcome of the kind of comparisons embodied in Equation (4.1) are different for different groups of people, and it is one of the challenges of small business research to clarify why this variation exists.

It is against the background of the discussion in this chapter, which has focused on the *individuals* who move into self-employment, that attention turns in Chapter 5 to empirical work on firm formation activity, where the primary focus is on the *organisation*.

5   Variations in formation activity

Introduction

In this chapter variations in business births across countries and regions are considered in the context of the analytical approach to formations outlined in Chapter 4. In the remainder of this section a snapshot picture of international differences in formation rates is provided. The focus then moves to an analysis of differences across regions and industry, using UK data. These latter differences are examined with the help of Value Added Tax registration statistics. It cannot of course be assumed that generalisations to other countries can be made from UK data, but it would be surprising if some of the underlying factors influencing formation in the United Kingdom were not also at work in other developed countries. The next section provides a way of thinking about the determinants of variations in formations. In the third section, the results of some empirical studies are considered. The final section concludes the chapter.

In considering formation rates it is helpful to bear in mind some preliminary measurement issues. First, the dating of a 'formation' is not without ambiguity. Should it be equated with (for example) the start of trading or the start of production, or employment? If the start of trading is chosen, does this mean the date of the very first transaction, whatever its size, or the date at which a specified minimum level of sales is achieved? Similar ambiguities surround the 'start' of production and employment. In reality, investigators usually have a definition imposed on them by the available data, but such a definition needs to be made explicit.

Second, any analysis of formation activity requires formation data to be normalised by some scaling factor. The two options most commonly used are, first, the stock of businesses at the beginning of the period under consideration, the 'opening stock', and second, some measure of the labour force or population, again at the beginning of the period. The choice of measure will depend on the purpose of the exercise. The opening stock of businesses will be the most appropriate measure if the concern is with variations in the extent to which the business sector is changing and rejuvenating itself. This way of measuring the birth rate is sometimes referred to as the 'ecological' approach (Armington and Acs 2002). A labour force or population measure – designated the 'labour market' approach by Armington and Acs (2002) – makes sense if the focus is on variations in the propensity of different groups of people to set up in business. The use of different scaling factors may of course give different results (see for example the study by Keeble and Walker 1994), a consequence which is nevertheless consistent with the fact that the two birth rates tend to be fairly strongly correlated.[1]

Third, even when specification of the formation rate has been selected, there is still a choice to be made between *gross* and *net* specifications. The latter is calculated after deaths have been deducted. Some data on the net formation rate for the United Kingdom are presented later.

International differences in formation

The most comprehensive data set for international comparisons is the *Global Entrepreneurship Monitor* database referred to in Chapter 4 (Minniti et al. 2006: 16–21). Table 5.1 presents *GEM* data on early-stage entrepreneurial activity (ESEA) – expressed as a percentage of the 18–64 population in thirty-five countries in 2004. It ranks countries from the highest to the lowest involvement in such activity.

Total ESEA in Table 5.1 is made up of, first, nascent entrepreneurial activity, measured by the numbers actively engaged in starting-up businesses in which they had an ownership stake but where no wages or salaries had been paid for more than three months, and second, owner managers of newly established businesses who have paid wages or salaries for more than three months, but less than forty-two months. The second and third columns of Table 5.1 provide data on the extent of these two elements in the adult population. A few individuals are involved in both sub-categories of ESEA, but they are counted only once in the total in the first column. Hence for a number of countries, this total is less than the sum of the second and third columns (see Minniti et al. 2006: 19).

The data are based on surveys of a representative sample of the population in each country but they must be regarded as subject to a margin of error. Also, it should be stressed that the data in the table relate to one year only, although the evidence suggests that cross-country differences in new business activity are fairly consistent over time (Acs et al. 2005: 16).

It is clear from Table 5.1 that there are very wide variations in the extent of ESEA across the thirty-five countries studied, ranging from 25 per cent of the adult working population in Venezuela and 21 per cent in Thailand, to around 2 per cent in Japan and Hungary (the average was 8.4 per cent). The table also shows that there is considerable variation in the relative importance of nascent entrepreneurship and new business owners, although in the majority of countries, the former dominates.

The explanation of the figures in Table 5.1 represents a huge research challenge on which there is still much work to be done. There are however some substantive results on international differences in *self-employment rates*. Some of

Table 5.1 Early-stage entrepreneurial activity in 35 countries, ranked by the percentage of the adult population engaged in such activity, 2005[a]

Early-stage entrepreneurial activity as % of adult population

Country	Total	Nascent entrepreneurial activity	New business owners
Venezuela	25.00	18.80	7.50
Thailand	20.70	9.70	13.10
New Zealand	17.60	9.40	10.00
Jamaica	17.00	10.50	6.70
China	13.70	5.60	9.40
United States	12.40	8.80	5.20
Brazil	11.30	3.30	8.20
Chile	11.10	6.00	5.30
Australia	10.90	6.50	4.70
Iceland	10.70	8.50	2.70
Ireland	9.80	5.70	4.70
Argentina	9.50	5.90	3.90
Canada	9.30	6.60	3.60
Norway	9.20	4.40	5.20
Singapore	7.20	3.90	3.70
Latvia	6.60	4.20	2.80
Greece	6.50	5.20	1.60
United Kingdom	6.20	3.40	2.90
Croatia	6.10	4.10	2.50
Switzerland	6.10	2.60	3.70
Mexico	5.90	4.60	1.40
Spain	5.70	2.40	3.40
France	5.40	4.70	0.70
Germany	5.40	3.10	2.70
Austria	5.30	3.00	2.40
South Africa	5.10	3.60	1.70
Finland	5.00	3.10	1.90
Italy	4.90	2.90	2.30
Denmark	4.80	2.40	2.40
Netherlands	4.40	2.50	1.90
Slovenia	4.40	3.00	1.40
Sweden	4.00	1.70	2.50
Belgium	3.90	2.90	1.20
Japan	2.20	1.10	1.10
Hungary	1.90	1.10	0.80
Average	**8.40**	**5.00**	**3.90**

Source: From Table 2, p. 18, *Global Entrepreneurship Monitor 2005 Executive Report* © 2006 Maria Minniti with William D. Bygrave and Erkko Autio, Babson College and London Business School (www.gemconsortium.org). Reproduced with permission.

Note: [a] See text for an explanation of why the first column is not always the sum of the following two.

the results of this work are worth noting here, although it should be remembered that self-employment and formation rates are far from perfectly correlated.[2] Parker and Robson (2004) have examined international differences in the former rate among OECD countries. They found that two key explanatory variables were average income tax rates (a positive and significant effect on self-employment) and the ratio of unemployment benefit to earnings (a significant and negative effect).

The effect of the tax rate may be a reflection of the more relaxed tax regime that exists under self-employment: as the tax rate rises, so individuals will be more attracted to such a regime. And of course the higher the unemployment benefit:earnings ratio is, the lower the incentive to enter own account activity in order to maintain income levels when redundancy occurs or is threatened. Such factors fit in well with the discussion of the formation decision in Chapter 4. Parker and Robson's (2004) work confirms that the self-employment rate is amenable to manipulation by financial levers, an important consideration for policymakers.

In earlier international comparisons among OECD countries, Acs et al. (1994) provide some empirical support for arguing that the self-employment rate is also affected by underlying macroeconomic and demographic forces. They found that this rate falls with: economic development, measured for example by gross national product (GNP) per capita; a rise in the female participation rate; the relative growth of the manufacturing sector; and the level of individualism in the economy. Parker and Robson (2004) however found little evidence for the influence of these kinds of macroeconomic or demographic variables – apart from the female participation rate – in their study. It should also be noted that the OECD countries are all advanced in economic terms; it is unclear how the analysis would change if a wider sample of countries were to be examined.

There is one factor not considered directly in either of the two studies reported in the previous paragraphs. It may be described as the 'cultural environment' for entrepreneurship (for a discussion, see OECD 1998: 50). This term captures, inter alia, social attitudes to business activity, success and failure. Because this environment is very difficult to measure, it does not typically figure in empirical work, yet it may be of critical importance in explaining international differences in formation rates.

Differences across regions and industries: the case of the United Kingdom

In this section the focus is on the United Kingdom and on data generated by VAT requirements for businesses to register. In effect, formation is equated with VAT registration. This assumed equivalence is not entirely satisfactory (see below), but it does enable access to a set of data, which, in its own terms, is robust.

UK businesses must register for VAT if their turnover reaches a threshold level – £61,000 in 2006. The resultant registration data have the advantage that they are readily available and provide comprehensive spatial and industrial coverage of registrations. They are also available from 1980.

The disadvantages of VAT registration statistics – they are generated by a taxation requirement imposed on businesses rather than by the needs of applied economic research – as a measure of firm births are well rehearsed (see for example Daly 1990; Storey 1994: 50–1). Firms are not required to register until they reach the threshold level of annual turnover, although they may choose to do so. Thus many very small firms are excluded from the VAT data: at the beginning of 2004, for example the 1.8 million businesses on the VAT register represented just 42 per cent of the official estimate of the total number of businesses in the United Kingdom (Department of Trade and Industry 2005). Registration may also sometimes result from a business reorganisation or a change of ownership, rather than from a birth.

For all these reasons, Storey (1994: 51) has rightly concluded that 'In only the broadest sense . . . can the number of businesses which are newly registered for VAT . . . be regarded as an indicator of the number of new business starts in any particular year'. Nevertheless, Keeble and Walker (1994: 411–12) have argued that, at least in respect of spatial analyses, the data 'represents the most up-to-date, comprehensive, reasonably long-term and spatially disaggregated data set currently available'. When it comes to looking at variations over time, it is important to be aware of the possibility that the commencement of trading or the taking-on of the first employee and VAT registration may not occur at the same time (Johnson and Conway 1997). The Bank of England (2004: 10) has also shown that data on the opening of business start-up bank accounts may give a rather different picture from the registration data.[3] The picture is further complicated by the fact that the VAT threshold has also changed over time, although in broad terms it has moved with inflation.

Deregistration data (also used below) present problems when used as an indicator of deaths. Many of these problems however are the mirror image of those relating to the use of registrations as a measure of births, and are not further considered here.

The rest of the chapter will refer to births (or formations) and deaths. Unless otherwise stated, these terms relate, respectively, to registrations and deregistrations. The 'stock' of businesses is the total number of VAT registered businesses.

Tables 5.2A and 5.2B summarise variations in birth rates across broad industrial sectors and regions in 2004. Although data for only one year are shown, it is unlikely that there are significant year to year fluctuations in the general picture presented in the tables.

The industrial data are normalised by business stock figures. They show a considerable concentration of births and deaths in just two sectors: Wholesaling, retail and repairs, and Real estate, renting and business activities together account for well over 50 per cent of both total births and total deaths. They account for slightly less of the total stock. The birth *rate* is highest (by a significant margin) in Hotels and restaurants, and Real estate, renting and business

Table 5.2A Births and deaths by industrial sector, UK, 2004

Industrial sector	Stock		Births		Deaths		Birth rate[a]	Death rate[a]	Net birth rate[a]
	No.	% of total	No.	% of total	No.	% of total			
Agriculture, forestry and fishing and fishing	145,780	8.0	3,720	2.1	8,595	4.8	2.55	5.90	−3.34
Mining and quarrying, utilities	1,820	0.1	190	0.1	240	0.1	10.44	13.19	−2.75
Manufacturing	156,035	8.6	9,865	5.4	13,915	7.8	6.32	8.92	−2.60
Wholesale, retail and repairs	388,425	21.4	36,610	20.2	37,300	20.8	9.43	9.60	−0.18
Construction	202,515	11.1	21,860	12.1	18,445	10.3	10.79	9.11	1.69
Hotels and restaurants	127,150	7.0	19,935	11.0	17,190	9.6	15.68	13.52	2.16
Transport, storage and communication	78,705	4.3	9,255	5.1	8,185	4.6	11.76	10.40	1.36
Financial intermediation	18,890	1.0	1,650	0.9	1,760	1.0	8.73	9.32	−0.58
Real estate, renting and business activities	524,435	28.8	65,645	36.2	58,145	32.4	12.52	11.09	1.43
Public administration, other services	147,290	8.1	10,475	5.8	13,885	7.7	7.11	9.43	−2.32
Education, health and social work	26,790	1.5	2,195	1.2	1,685	0.9	8.19	6.29	1.90
Total[b]	1,817,835	100.0	181,400	100.0	179,345	100.0	9.98	9.87	0.11

Source: Derived from VAT statistics published by the Small Business Service (www.sbs.gov.uk)

Notes: [a] As a percentage of the stock of registered businesses at the beginning of the year.
 [b] The totals for industry (Table 5.2A) and for the regions (Table 5.2B) are not identical because of rounding errors.

Table 5.2B Births and deaths by region, UK, 2004

| Region | Stock | | Births | | Deaths | | Birth rate[a] | Death rate[a] | Net birth rate[a] | per 10,000 adult residents | | | |
	No.	% of total	No.	% of total	No.	% of total				Stock	Births	Deaths	Net births
North East	45,610	2.5	4,290	2.4	4,090	2.3	9.41	8.97	0.44	220.9	20.8	19.8	1.0
North West	172,080	9.5	17,640	9.7	16,890	9.4	10.25	9.82	0.44	314.2	32.2	30.8	1.4
Yorks/ Humberside	130,345	7.2	12,835	7.1	12,230	6.8	9.85	9.38	0.46	322.0	31.7	30.2	1.5
East Midlands	124,300	6.8	12,205	6.7	11,330	6.3	9.82	9.12	0.70	360.0	35.4	32.8	2.5
West Midlands	152,280	8.4	14,855	8.2	14,975	8.4	9.76	9.83	-0.08	357.3	34.9	35.1	-0.3
East of England	183,590	10.1	17,580	9.7	17,495	9.8	9.58	9.53	0.05	416.0	39.8	39.6	0.2
London	285,720	15.7	35,460	19.6	35,925	20.0	12.41	12.57	-0.16	477.3	59.2	60.0	-0.8
South East	287,055	15.8	28,360	15.6	28,245	15.8	9.88	9.84	0.04	439.8	43.5	43.3	0.2
South West	170,430	9.4	15,310	8.4	14,970	8.4	8.98	8.78	0.20	415.0	37.3	36.5	0.8
Wales	79,760	4.4	6,900	3.8	6,650	3.7	8.65	8.34	0.31	335.1	29.0	27.9	1.1
Scotland	127,280	7.0	11,845	6.5	11,980	6.7	9.31	9.41	-0.11	307.2	28.6	28.9	-0.3
N Ireland	59,375	3.3	4,140	2.3	4,595	2.6	6.97	7.74	-0.77	447.4	31.2	34.6	-3.4
UK[b]	1,817,820	100.0	181,415	100.0	179,370	100.0	9.98	9.87	0.11	377.2	37.7	37.2	0.4

Source: Derived from VAT statistics published by the Small Business Service (www.sbs.gov.uk)

Notes: [a] As a percentage of the stock of registered businesses at the beginning of the year.
  [b] The totals for industry (Table 5.2A) and for the regions (Table 5.2B) are not identical because of rounding errors.

activities, two sectors where small-scale activity can be very efficient. In all sectors, the *net* birth rate is far less than the birth rate because of the loss of businesses through deaths. In six sectors, there is a net loss, with births being more than offset by deaths. It is Hotels and restaurants that has the biggest net birth rate.

The industrial data have not been normalised by a labour force/population measure because of the difficulty of relating the VAT sectoral classifications to those on which labour force statistics are based.[4] (See Creedy and Johnson 1983 for a study that normalises the data in this way.)[5]

The regional breakdown of formations (Table 5.2B) is however normalised by both opening stock and population. Whichever measure is used, there is clearly wide variation between regions in both births and deaths and a considerable concentration of formation activity: the South East including London has about 35 per cent of all births (and about the same percentage of deaths).

Two other features of Tables 5.2A and 5.2B should be noted. First, there is a very high positive correlation between the birth and the death rates. The correlation between the two based on the industrial breakdown in Table 5.2A is 0.80. In Table 5.2B, the correlation is 0.96 when the stock of businesses is used as the denominator in the birth rate calculation and 0.98 with the population figure. This positive correlation reflects the fact that births and deaths are not independent: for example, a birth may lead to the death of another through the competitive process; a death may lead to a birth by providing market 'space' for a newcomer. And of course, the normal process of businesses ageing and dying will ensure that after an appropriate lag, death will follow birth for many, if not nearly all enterprises.[6] As Marshall (1920: 263) says of businesses, 'sooner or later age tells on them all'. These relationships between births and deaths are further explored in Chapter 7 when the competitive implications of small firms are considered.

Second, there is very substantial turbulence. Turbulence is a measure of the overall scale of 'to-ing' and 'fro-ing' of businesses (Beesley and Hamilton 1984). For current purposes it may be measured by the sum of the birth and death rates. The UK figures in Table 5.2B show that in 2004, turbulence was 20 per cent of the opening business stock. Yet out of all this turbulence, there was a *net* increase of just one-tenth of 1 per cent.

Factors influencing formation

There is now an extensive literature that seeks to explain variations in formation rates across regions. It is clear from these studies that the causes of these variations are complex. At least two approaches to analysing the variations have been adopted in the literature. The first is the 'accounting' approach which seeks to decompose the data into various components. The second is the economic modelling of formations. The accounting approach has been utilised primarily on the analysis of spatial variations. Both approaches are examined below.

The accounting approach

A basic framework

This approach has been utilised in Johnson (1983), Storey and Johnson (1987) and, most recently, in Johnson (2004). This section draws heavily on the last of these articles.[7] The starting point is the formal expression of two key birth rates, where the numbers of births are normalised by the stock of businesses. First consider sector *i* in region *r*. The formation rate for this sector (ignoring time subscripts) may be defined as follows:

$$f_{i,r} = \frac{VR_{i,r}}{VS_{i,r}} \quad \text{where}$$

$VR_{i,r}$ = the annual number of VAT registrations in sector *i* in region *r*; and

$VS_{i,r}$ = the stock of registered VAT businesses at the beginning of the year in sector *i* in region *r*.

The formation rate in sector *i* *in the country as a whole* (here the United Kingdom), $f_{i,UK}$, may be defined as

$$f_{i,UK} = \frac{\displaystyle\sum_{r=1}^{m} VR_{i,r}}{\displaystyle\sum_{r=1}^{m} VS_{i,r}} \quad \text{where}$$

m = the number of regions.

The following analysis utilises these formation rates in a comparison of the actual number of births in region *r*, denoted here as A_r, and the 'National Standard' number of births in region *r*, denoted here as NS_r. The latter may be defined as the number of births region *r* would have had if the stock of registered businesses in the region had displayed the same industrial distribution as that in the United Kingdom as whole, and if the birth rate in each sector had also been the same as that in the United Kingdom. More formally,

$$NS_r = \sum_{i=1}^{n} \left(\frac{VS_r VS_{i,UK} f_{i,UK}}{VS_{UK}} \right)$$

where the notation is as before, and

VS_r = total stock of businesses in region *r*;
$VS_{i,UK}$ = UK stock of businesses in sector *i*;

VS_{UK} = total UK stock of businesses (in all sectors); and
n = number of sectors

A_r minus NS_r may be defined as the regional 'deficit' where it is negative and as the regional 'surplus' where it is positive.

Some data

Table 5.3 provides some data on the NS_r / A_r ratio. (A ratio of one indicates that the number of formations that *would be expected* on the basis of national data is the same as the *actual* number.) The results for all sectors show that only London and the South East have had ratios that have been consistently greater than one over the period 1994–2001. In London, the 'excess' has been very substantial in all years. In two further regions, the ratio is one or above in specified years: in the North West between 1996 and 2001 and in the East of England in 1995, 1997, 2000 and 2001.

Not surprisingly, the exclusion of Agriculture has the effect of significantly lowering the ratio for London and the South East – in the case of the latter, taking it marginally below one in 1999 and 2000 – and raising it for the South West, Wales, Scotland and Northern Ireland (see Johnson 2004 for the detail). These changes reflect the fact that the UK formation rate is very low in Agriculture – as Table 5.2A shows, this rate was only 2.6 per cent in 2004 compared with 10.0 per cent for all sectors – and that in London and the South East, Agriculture is very underrepresented in terms of its share of the stock of registered businesses, whereas in the areas where the ratio rises, it accounts for a substantially higher share. In the United Kingdom as a whole, Agriculture accounted for around 8 per cent of the stock of registered businesses in 2004; in Northern Ireland it was over a third. The exclusion of Agriculture does not however fundamentally alter the picture as far as the A_r / NS_r ratio is concerned. London continues to have higher than expected formation activity; and this is also true for the South East except in 1999 and 2000. The results in Table 5.3 are broadly consistent with those obtained for the early 1980s by Storey and Johnson (1987).

Now the *difference* between A_r and NS_r may be broken down into a Structural Component, S_r, and a Formation Component, F_r, as follows

$$S_r = \sum_{i=1}^{n} \left(VS_{ir} - VS_r \frac{VS_{i,UK}}{VS_{UK}} \right) f_{i,UK}$$

$$F_r = \sum_{i=1}^{N} VS_{ir} \left(f_{ir} - f_{i,UK} \right)$$

Thus the Structural Component shows how many new registrations would be generated by applying the national formation rate in each sector to the difference between the actual stock of registered businesses in each sector and what that

Table 5.3 The NS_R/A_R ratio: UK regions, 1994–2001

Region	1994	1995	1996	1997	1998	1999	2000	2001	Average 1994–2001
North East	**0.98**	**0.92**	**0.92**	**0.87**	**0.88**	**0.93**	**0.92**	**0.91**	**0.92**
Ex Agriculture	*0.97*	*0.92*	*0.92*	*0.87*	*0.88*	*0.93*	*0.92*	*0.92*	*0.92*
North West	**0.98**	**0.98**	**1.00**	**1.02**	**1.03**	**1.05**	**1.04**	**1.03**	**1.01**
Ex Agriculture	*0.96*	*0.96*	*0.98*	*1.00*	*1.01*	*1.03*	*1.02*	*1.01*	*1.00*
Yorks/Humberside	**0.92**	**0.90**	**0.91**	**0.88**	**0.88**	**0.91**	**0.93**	**0.95**	**0.91**
Ex Agriculture	*0.92*	*0.91*	*0.91*	*0.89*	*0.88*	*0.92*	*0.93*	*0.96*	*0.91*
East Midlands	**0.94**	**0.95**	**0.94**	**0.94**	**0.94**	**0.94**	**0.98**	**0.99**	**0.95**
Ex Agriculture	*0.95*	*0.96*	*0.95*	*0.95*	*0.95*	*0.94*	*0.99*	*0.99*	*0.96*
West Midlands	**0.96**	**0.95**	**0.94**	**0.89**	**0.97**	**0.98**	**0.96**	**0.98**	**0.95**
Ex Agriculture	*0.96*	*0.95*	*0.93*	*0.88*	*0.97*	*0.97*	*0.96*	*0.98*	*0.95*
East of England	**0.98**	**1.00**	**0.98**	**1.02**	**0.98**	**0.97**	**1.02**	**1.00**	**0.99**
Ex Agriculture	*0.97*	*0.99*	*0.97*	*1.01*	*0.96*	*0.96*	*1.01*	*0.99*	*0.98*
London	**1.30**	**1.33**	**1.32**	**1.31**	**1.34**	**1.28**	**1.25**	**1.20**	**1.29**
Ex Agriculture	*1.20*	*1.23*	*1.23*	*1.21*	*1.24*	*1.19*	*1.16*	*1.11*	*1.20*
South East	**1.09**	**1.08**	**1.07**	**1.09**	**1.06**	**1.04**	**1.03**	**1.05**	**1.06**
Ex Agriculture	*1.05*	*1.03*	*1.03*	*1.04*	*1.01*	*0.99*	*0.99*	*1.00*	*1.02*
South West	**0.90**	**0.85**	**0.89**	**0.91**	**0.91**	**0.94**	**0.93**	**0.92**	**0.91**
Ex Agriculture	*0.94*	*0.89*	*0.94*	*0.96*	*0.96*	*0.98*	*0.98*	*0.97*	*0.95*
Wales	**0.76**	**0.76**	**0.76**	**0.73**	**0.71**	**0.74**	**0.75**	**0.77**	**0.75**
Ex Agriculture	*0.86*	*0.85*	*0.86*	*0.81*	*0.80*	*0.83*	*0.86*	*0.87*	*0.85*
Scotland	**0.92**	**0.93**	**0.91**	**0.92**	**0.87**	**0.89**	**0.87**	**0.92**	**0.90**
Ex Agriculture	*0.97*	*0.97*	*0.96*	*0.97*	*0.92*	*0.94*	*0.92*	*0.98*	*0.95*
N Ireland	**0.63**	**0.68**	**0.67**	**0.63**	**0.60**	**0.60**	**0.57**	**0.63**	**0.63**
Ex Agriculture	*0.72*	*0.79*	*0.78*	*0.74*	*0.73*	*0.76*	*0.73*	*0.80*	*0.76*

Source: Johnson (2004), used with permission of Blackwell Publishing. The table is based on analyses of VAT registrations available from the UK Small Business Service (see http//www.sbs.gov.uk).

stock would have been if the region had had the same industrial structure of registered businesses as the United Kingdom as a whole. The Formation Component, on the other hand, shows the number of registrations that would be generated by applying the difference between the regional and national formation rates in each sector to the regional stock of businesses.

Table 5.4 presents data for 1994–2001 on the Formation and Structural Components when Agriculture is included in the calculations. The shaded figures relate to those where the A_r/NS_r is equal to, or greater than, one. The overall picture varies considerably from region to region. In two of the deficit regions, the North East, and Yorkshire and Humberside (except 2001), the Formation Component dominates. In three further deficit regions, East Midlands, Wales and Northern Ireland, it is the Structural Component that consistently accounts for the majority of the difference between A_r and NS_r. (In Wales however there are a number of years where the two components are of a similar magnitude.) In the West Midlands, the South West and Scotland, the Structural Component also dominates in all but one or two years.

In those regions where A_r/NS_r is greater than one in some or all of the years, the picture is also varied. In the South East, the Structural Component considerably outweighs the Formation counterpart in all years whereas in London, the latter is more important in all but two of the years. No clear pattern emerges in the East of England. In the North West, the Formation Component dominates in all years.

It is clear from the data that changing the relative position of a region constitutes a significant policy challenge: Table 5.3 shows that no region has sustained a continuous year on year improvement in its relative position over the whole period. The two regions that started the period with the lowest ratio (Wales and Northern Ireland) saw no significant improvement in their relative position over the period. The high correlation found by Johnson (2004) between the early 1980s data used by Storey and Johnson (1987) and those presented in Table 5.3 further emphasises the long run nature of the challenge for regions seeking to raise relatively low formation rates.

The accounting approach: a review

It is important to be aware of some of the limitations of the 'decomposition' technique. Two may be mentioned. First, the technique is essentially an 'accounting' tool that does not seek to identify causal relationships. It may however provide hints on these relationships. Second, it treats the Structural and Formation Components as independent elements when in fact there may be some interdependencies between them. For example, the structural characteristics of a region may influence formation activity in that region. One reason for this is that industries differ in the scope that they offer for both upstream and downstream small firm activity and hence formations. Conversely, formation activity is one of the mechanisms by which the structure of a region is shaped, with growing industries attracting new firms and declining industries shedding firms.

Table 5.4 Formation (F) and structural (S) components, UK regions, 1994–2001

Region	1994		1995		1996		1997		1998		1999		2000		2001	
	F	S	F	S	F	S	F	S	F	S	F	S	F	S	F	S
North East	-65	-40	-296	-43	-321	-57	-524	-94	-475	-114	-259	-49	-292	-64	-331	-46
North West	-305	-50	-333	-41	-49	-26	376	-85	493	1	617	175	588	156	388	124
Yorks/ Humberside	-611	-404	-798	-381	-712	-418	-1,044	-530	-1,086	-561	-726	-357	-574	-392	-194	-382
East Midlands	-195	-488	-143	-441	-249	-460	-163	-562	-148	-595	-327	-434	220	-462	241	-407
West Midlands	-167	-437	-257	-379	-523	-389	-1,213	-506	125	-554	97	-417	-155	-449	142	-398
East of England	-501	98	-223	187	-524	173	50	287	-751	292	-702	201	167	201	-168	233
London	3,748	3,777	4,654	3,394	4,707	3,594	4,737	3,982	5,718	4,239	4,712	3,455	3,857	3,706	2,475	3,234
South East	679	1,552	307	1,604	56	1,725	321	2,096	-534	2,178	-677	1,663	-785	1,726	-315	1,627
South West	-798	-836	-1486	-848	-772	-894	-483	-952	-461	-996	-191	-844	-262	-861	-532	-742
Wales	-879	-1,051	-857	-1,022	-794	-1,091	-1,138	-1,211	-1,245	-1,275	-1,065	-1,069	-924	-1,122	-823	-1,007
Scotland	-276	-752	-169	-710	-348	-753	-256	-847	-836	-924	-668	-797	-882	-829	-270	-713
N Ireland	-639	-1364	-414	-1317	-447	-1,401	-668	-1,575	-801	-1,688	-813	-1,523	-966	-1,606	-620	-1,520

Source: Johnson (2004), used with permission of Blackwell Publishing. The table is based on analyses of VAT registrations available from the UK Small Business Service (http://www.sbs.gov.uk/).

The limitations of the data referred to earlier must also be firmly borne in mind. A further potential limitation arises from the level of industrial aggregation in the data. It is unclear how sensitive the results are to the level chosen.

Notwithstanding the above deficiencies, the technique provides a number of useful initial insights into regional differences in births and pointers to the direction for future research. First, the results point to a wide variety of experience across regions and in some regions, over time. In some cases the results are sensitive to whether or not Agriculture is excluded. This variation highlights the complexity of the processes involved and suggests that different policy responses are likely to be appropriate in different regions and at different times. The application of a standard policy 'package' across regions is likely to be misguided.

Second, the data suggest that the explanation for relatively low birth rates is likely to vary across regions. Two contrasting examples may help to illustrate this point. In the North East, it is clear from Table 5.4 that a key reason behind this region's birth rate 'deficit' is that, *sector by sector*, the birth rate tends to be lower than elsewhere. This in turn raises the question of how far the North East's relatively low formation rate in a sector is due to region-wide influences, e.g. a culture that is less supportive of business formation generally, and how far to sector specific differences, relating for example to market opportunities, supply constraints and agglomeration economies. The central policy issue here is the question whether these influences are amenable to efficient intervention.

In contrast, the East Midlands deficit is dominated by the Structural Component. (This is true even when Agriculture is excluded.) In this region, rather more attention might be given to why the structure of industry is as it is and to the question of whether this structure might be adapted by policy measures. Care is needed here: the industrial structure of a region is a reflection of a wide range of influences and it may be inappropriate to seek to alter that structure simply to raise the formation rate. Careful analysis of the reasons for the current structure and of the implications of seeking to alter it is necessary.

Finally, it is important to note the dominance of London. Its A_r/NS_r ratio (see Table 5.3) is very significantly higher than that for any other region in the United Kingdom, even when adjustment is made for Agriculture. Furthermore, the capital has a substantial advantage in both structural and formation terms when it comes to business births. This in turn reflects the financial and other attractions of a capital city as a centre for entrepreneurial activity. No other region is likely to be able to match these unique advantages and it would be a mistake to endeavour to emulate the record of region that is clearly a special case.

As suggested above, the accounting approach does not provide *explanations* of regional differences (although it may hint at them). It is this challenge that the next section explores.

Modelling formation activity

In thinking about how formation activity might be modelled, it may be helpful to start with a market – defined in both spatial and product terms – that is in equilibrium, with no entry or exit, no excess profits, and no opportunity for cost reductions or innovation. Such a situation is a substantial abstraction from the dynamic nature of economic activity, but it serves as a starting point. Changes to this equilibrium may now be examined.

Increases in demand

The demand for new businesses in this rarified world is a *derived* demand; it is the *consequence* of the increase in demand for the output of existing firms. This increase will typically cause these existing firms to raise their output, and/or prices in the short run. Such increases in demand may arise for a number of reasons, including a rise in incomes, changes in tastes or policy developments. They may also result from the closure of firms. As a result of such a demand stimulus, profits will increase. This in turn will make the market more attractive to potential entrants. Formation activity is therefore likely to increase.

The responsiveness (or 'elasticity') of business formation with respect to market demand will however vary across product and spatial markets and over time, since the relevant supply function of would-be business founders may differ. This variation will reflect differences in the way in which any proportionate increase in demand is distributed across different *types* of actual or potential suppliers: entirely new businesses, cross entrants diversifying from other industries, and existing firms. These variations will reflect differences in the relative costs of these sources of additional supply.

The relative height of entry barriers facing the different types of entrant may also differ across markets. In addition, there are likely to be differences in the optimal size of firm. This in turn will generate differences in *how many* new firms are formed for a given increase in demand. It is interesting to note in this context that Keeble and Walker (1994) showed that the impact of increased demand, measured by population growth, generated more formations in services than in production industries. Differing policy environments too may cause variations in impact.

Increases in supply

An increase in the supply of would-be founders – generated for example by training schemes to encourage people to think about starting up – will also lead (other things being equal) to an increase in formation activity. Again, however, a given proportionate increase in supply of founders would be unlikely to translate into exactly the same response in terms of new businesses in all markets, because of differing demand conditions.

Implications and limitations

The above paragraphs make a distinction between a disequilibrating *shift* on the demand (supply) side, and the *conditions* of supply (demand) that influence the impact of such a shift. Such a distinction, which does not feature strongly in the literature on formation, is helpful to bear in mind in interpreting the empirical work in this area.

This kind of analysis, based on standard textbook microeconomics, is however somewhat mechanistic in its approach, and does not capture the fact that some new firms may themselves play a key role in generating demand increases, for example by opening up new markets for existing goods and services or by developing new ones. Indeed by their formation such firms may have a 'multiplier' effect on births if they generate opportunities for other firms to exploit. They may also be responsible for introducing the kind of cost reduction through process innovation and general efficiency gains that leads to own account activity becoming attractive. Of course existing firms may perform these functions of the Schumpeterian entrepreneur. The relative importance of new firms in performing these functions will vary from industry to industry.

Empirical studies

Not surprisingly, empirical studies have identified a wide range of potential influences: in the review by Keeble et al. (1993: 31–3), for example, over thirty such influences were identified. At the risk of oversimplification the key influences may be grouped under two broad headings: those that operate primarily on the demand for new firms, and those that affect their supply. Policy initiatives may affect either or both demand and supply, depending on the nature of the intervention.

Demand side factors

Investigators looking at spatial differences in formation across space and over time have tried to capture shifts in demand for output through such variables as population, gross domestic product (GDP) and household income. Keeble and Walker (1994) for example found that population change was a significant and positive explanatory variable in explaining county variations in births.[8] In his analysis of the UK formation rate over the period 1980–90, Robson (1996b) identified the *rate of growth* of real GDP as having a significant positive effect. A much more direct measure of the impact of output demand on prospects for own account activity is of course the perceived returns to own business activity. This measure was used successfully by Creedy and Johnson (1983) to explain cross-industry variations in formation activity in manufacturing.

The industry mix has also been treated as a demand side influence in some studies (e.g. Johnson and Parker 1996). The reasoning here is that the share of output going to services (one measure of industry mix) is likely to reflect the share of services in demand, and that the demand for services is likely to be relatively more congenial to new start-ups, since it is more frequently satisfied by small-scale activity.

Supply side factors

On the supply side, a key concern has been with measures that seek to capture the availability of paid employment opportunities. Most attention here has focused on the unemployment rate. The argument here is that as the unemployment rate rises, so would-be founders are more likely to be 'pushed' into setting up in business, because the opportunity cost of working on an own account basis, in terms of forgone earnings, falls (paid employment opportunities are fewer). As Chapter 4 pointed out, this 'push' effect of unemployment is much debated. One of the difficulties of using the unemployment measure in empirical work is that it may also pick up demand side effects. Thus while a rise in unemployment may provide a greater incentive for people to set up in business because of reduced paid employment opportunities, it may also signal a fall in market prospects. Empirical work will of course pick up only the net effect of these influences, and it is therefore hardly surprising to find a lack of consistency in the results of empirical studies on the effects of unemployment. Johnson and Parker (1996) found a significant *negative* effect of unemployment on regional formations (after a two year lag). Robson (1996b) similarly found a negative unemployment effect. Yet in their international study, Reynolds et al. (1994) found some countries where unemployment had a broadly positive effect on regional births (see also Acs et al. 1994). Black et al. (1996) also detected a positive impact of unemployment on formations in their study of VAT registrations, 1974–90. The ambiguity of the impact of unemployment has been much debated in the literature (see for example Storey 1991).

Other measures of the tightness of the labour market have been tried. For example, Robson (1996b) uses vacancies, which he finds has a significant positive effect. This finding is consistent with his finding on unemployment; and with both measures being dominated by demand pressures. Creedy and Johnson (1983) use a direct measure of wages in paid employment in their cross industry study. The sign here is, as expected, negative. (The coefficient is significant.)

The failure to identify unambiguously a 'push' effect from poor labour market conditions in empirical studies designed to identify overall macro influences is of course fully consistent with the fact that *some* founders are motivated by the threat of actual or potential redundancy (see for example Johnson and Rodger 1983; Mason 1989).

Another supply side variable that has attracted a good deal of attention is the availability of finance. Black et al. (1996) show that increases in the amount of net housing wealth (the value of the owner-occupied stock less outstanding mortgages) increases formation activity. The argument here is that such wealth, which provides collateral, is likely to have a positive effect on the availability of bank lending. While Keeble and Walker (1994) find a positive effect of local house values on births, it should be noted that they use average house prices as their measure, apparently with no deduction for outstanding debt. In Robson (1996b), results supporting Black et al. (1996) were provided. In a parallel paper however (Robson 1996a), no positive relationship between net housing wealth and regional rates of firm formation was found. Indeed if anything the results in this paper suggest a negative relationship (see also Johnson and Parker 1996). One reason for doubt over the effect of net housing wealth is that it may also pick up demand side effects. Another problem is that founders of very small new businesses may typically be reluctant to borrow anything and that when they do, they do not obtain collateralised finance (evidence by Robert Cressy, quoted in Robson 1996a).[9] For such founders, net housing wealth may be largely irrelevant to the formation decision.

A number of studies have suggested certain population characteristics may have an impact on the supply of new businesses. First, evidence suggests that the rate of formation is higher in the more skilled or professional occupations (Barkham 1992).

Second, the incidence of formation activity appears to vary with age (although as indicated on p. 39, the entry rate for US white males is relatively stable between the mid-twenties and mid-forties, it shows significant variation outside that range: see Evans and Leighton 1989); gender (females have a lower propensity to go into business: see, for example, Cowling and Taylor 2001; Minniti et al. 2005); and ethnic origin (some groups are more likely to set up than others: Borjas 1986). Educational qualifications – clearly related to occupational structure – have also been explored although there is some ambiguity in the results of empirical work in this area (see for example Storey 1982: 106).

A number of possible explanations lie behind the fact that groups of individuals with certain characteristics have been found, historically, to have a higher propensity to set up in business. It may be for example that such individuals are relatively more responsive to demand increases. They may as a group be more market orientated and aware of potential opportunities. Again they may be relatively disadvantaged in the paid employment market, so that a given level of perceived self-employment returns seems relatively more attractive. Empirical work has not been able fully to disentangle these effects.

The size structure of local industry may affect formation activity from the supply side. A number of studies have shown that the spin-off rate of new firm founders tends to be higher in smaller plants/firms (e.g. Johnson and Cathcart 1979b; Gudgin and Fothergill 1984).[10] One reason for this is that employees in small businesses are more likely to come into contact with, and be more sensitive to, market opportunities that are relevant for small firms, and to be more familiar with small business operations. Thus a given increase in the demand for a particular product or service may generate more formations in contexts where there are relatively more small firm employees. It is also likely that if the number of small firms increases relatively, there will be greater awareness of small business opportunities. There may also be other arguments to suggest that the greater the relative share of small businesses, the higher the formation rate. Wages and security of employment tend to be lower in smaller businesses, hence (other things being equal) the attractions of a given own account business opportunity may appear greater for the small firm employee. Notwithstanding these arguments, the evidence on the effect of size structure on formation is mixed (see Keeble and Walker 1994).

Finally, the industry mix which was earlier proposed as a demand side element may also act on the supply side. Here the argument is that this mix will tend to capture the extent to which local industry acts as a 'seedbed' for would-be founders who are likely to come, disproportionately, from the service sector.

Policy intervention

Policy intervention may operate on the demand or supply sides. The management of aggregate demand is clearly a relevant influence on the former, although it should be noted that any change in demand may have both positive and negative effects on formation. Supply side measures include the encouragement of would-be founders to set up in business by the provision of training and/or advice, grants and loans, and subsidised premises, although there has been relatively little empirical work on the impact of such measures.

The general policy stance of central and local government may also affect formation, although Keeble and Walker (1994) found that their measure of this stance at local level – the percentage of Labour and (in the case of Scotland and Wales) nationalist councillors on a local authority – had mixed effects on formation rates. Robson (1996b) has explored the impact of income tax rates, the real interest rate and inflation, finding that all had a significant negative effect on formations, although it is unclear precisely what explanation lies behind these results.[11] Corporation tax had no discernible effect, nor did social benefits. (The latter is one measure of the financial alternative to self-employment returns.) Policy issues are further considered in Chapter 10.

Some puzzles

The empirical studies mentioned above are not without their puzzles. For example, Keeble and Walker (1994) utilise independent variables, which are significant in some of the equations but are not included in others. Why, for example, do they find that changes in GDP per head are highly significant in services, but that such changes are not included in the Production sector equation? There are also some puzzles over the same variables having different signs. Keeble and Walker's (1994) summary measure of the size distribution and their measure of the political stance of the local authority, have different signs in different equations. More generally, there are differences in the results across studies by different authors that require further investigation. For example, Robson (1996b) and Black et al. (1996), who both use VAT registration data for overlapping periods, each show a positive effect of net housing wealth on births (not found in Robson 1996a), yet they disagree on the effects of unemployment.

Concluding comment

This chapter has briefly reviewed some of the empirical work on firm formation. Fairly robust economic arguments can be presented for some of the results that have been obtained. At the same time it is important to acknowledge, and to seek an explanation for, the puzzles that are thrown up by the results. It is also important to note that the amount of variation in formation activity explained by most studies still leaves a good deal unexplained. There is still more work to do. Chapter 6 now moves a stage on, and looks at the survival and growth of new businesses.

6 Survival and growth

Introduction

This chapter moves on from the formation stage and considers two key issues for business development. Survival is examined in the next section and the growth of new firms in the third.

It is important to be explicit about the unit of analysis that is being examined. A *business* may continue to grow while the *individual* who owns and runs it may change. Indeed it may be precisely because such change occurs, that a business is able to survive and/or develop. Thus a particular individual may not last very long in business, but the business in which he or she has been involved continues. Conversely, someone may prosper in business by setting up and then closing down successive businesses. In this chapter most of the focus is on the business as the unit of analysis, although some attention is also paid to the individuals who enter own account activity and their subsequent progress.

Survival

Some data

The key question dealt with in this section is: why do so many businesses exit within a few years of start-up?

Chapter 4 showed that less than 50 per cent of businesses registered for VAT in the United Kingdom are still registered six years later and that a similar percentage applies to registrations of companies. Company registration data also provide some information on survival over the much longer term. They show that only 11 per cent of companies registered in 1950–4 were still on the books in March 2004, and that the percentage for those registered in the period 1900–9 was less than five (Department of Trade and Industry 2004a: 35). Thus nearly all companies have gone within a century.

VAT or company deregistration may not mean that the business ceases to exist. Some deregistrations may reflect reorganisation of an existing business, or in the case of companies, a decision to adopt another legal form.

For the United States, some data on the longevity of new businesses are provided by Audretsch (1995), who looked at the experience of over 11,000 new firms started up in manufacturing in 1976.[1] He showed that only 35 per cent of these firms were still 'live' within ten years, a percentage which is broadly consistent with UK data: for example, 31 per cent of UK registered companies in 1994 survived the ten years to 2004 (Department of Trade and Industry 2004a: 35). Evidence from Evans and Leighton (1989) suggests that around 49 per cent of the self-employed in the United States had abandoned that status by the sixth year after entering it. For further evidence see Caves (1998).

Survival tends to be positively associated with size. For example, in 1980 in the United Kingdom, the deregistration rate for firms registered for VAT was over five times higher for the smallest registered businesses (defined as those with a turnover of £13,000 or less in 1980), compared with the largest (more than £2 million in 1980) (from Ganguly 1985: 86). Dunne and Hughes (1994) show that in a sample of 2149 companies alive in 1980, 27 per cent of those with less than £1 million in assets had disappeared by 1985, whereas the figure for those of more than £64 million was 14 per cent. US evidence (Evans 1987) is supportive of this positive relationship between size and survival.

Interestingly however, the disappearance–size relationship between the two extreme size bands in the Dunne and Hughes (1994) study was not linear. If anything the data suggest that beyond the very smallest category (less than £1 million assets) the relationship between survival rates and size tends to follow an inverted U. It is also worth noting that a substantial proportion of disappearances were accounted for by take-over: 41 per cent in the case of those firms with under £1 million assets, and 72 per cent in the case of those with over £64 million assets. The relationship between size and exit rates varies across different types of exit.

In the United States, the work by Dunne et al. (1989) on manufacturing *plants* shows that the exit rate among those with 5–19 employees was more than double that for plants with more than 250 employees.[2] The proportion of plants in the smallest size band used by these authors – 5–19 employees – which exited between one and six years after first appearing was 41 per cent. This is lower than might be expected from the data so far presented, but it should be recognised that the very smallest firms were excluded, and that the sample is restricted to manufacturing. Some of these plants would also have been set up by well-established firms who might be expected to make fewer mistakes in their assessment (for example) of costs and demand, than the entirely new start-up.

It may be that size is proxying age, since the smallest firms tend also to be the youngest. Is it, for example, inexperience of the marketplace, rather than small size per se, that is generating exit? There are some a priori grounds for supposing that *both* size and age are likely to exert a positive influence on longevity. As far as size is concerned, it may be argued – following Geroski's (1995) argument – that it provides a measure, albeit an imperfect one, of the 'accumulation of basic competitive assets or skills'. Age is an indicator, inter alia, of the learning embodied in the plant's management. Both factors are likely to mean that the firm is better able to deal with any external shocks. On the empirical front, Dunne et al. (1989) show that at least for their US manufacturing plants, both age and size do in general have independent, negative effects on exit rates.[3] This evidence is confirmed in other work, such as the studies by Evans (1987) and Mata and Portugal (1994).

Not surprisingly, there is some evidence of an industry effect on exit, an effect that is discussed later.

Some explanations

Against this background it is appropriate now to return to the original puzzle posed by the data: why do so many firms exit so soon after entry?[4] Why is survival apparently more difficult than entry? Some people who set up in business may *intend* only to stay for a very short period. But probably for the majority of those who exit, their demise is, for them, premature.

Clues to a possible explanation lie in the empirical literature on entry. In his wide-ranging and careful review of this literature, Geroski (1995) has pointed out that entry barriers and profitability explain only a small amount of the variation in entry rates across industries. The absence of a strong relationship may partly reflect measurement difficulties, but Geroski's 'stylised result' from the entry literature is consistent with other findings. For example, there is evidence to suggest that at any given time, at least in manufacturing, a very substantial proportion of plants are operating at less than minimum efficient scale. Weiss (1991: 106) for example, drawing on both US and UK evidence, suggests that the output coming from sub-optimal plants typically accounts for between 48 and 58 per cent of the total. These figures translate into much higher percentages for the *number of firms* operating at sub-optimal level, because of the skewed distribution of firm sizes. Weiss's own view at the beginning of the 1990s, was that typically only about 5–10 per cent of firms in most industries would be operating at minimum efficient scale 'or anything like it' (Weiss 1991: xiv).

Almost certainly, the overwhelming majority of new firms will be operating sub-optimally. In the absence of compensating factors – such as the presence of a niche market or artificial protection from competition – such firms will be at a cost disadvantage from the start. Weiss's (1991) evidence is exclusively concerned with manufacturing, but it would be surprising if the general thrust of his findings did not also apply to services and construction.

One interpretation of these findings is that large numbers of entrants may be ignorant, at the time they enter, of the extent of the scale disadvantage they face, or if they are not, they may misjudge – overestimate – their ability to overcome that disadvantage by growing quickly enough to reach MES, or by developing some form of protection, before they are forced out of business. Some evidence that new firms typically overestimate their prospects together with some suggestions as to why this is the case have already been presented: see Chapter 4.

The fact that the overall exit rate is high among young businesses is of course consistent with there being some systematic explanation of why some businesses survive and others do not. This issue has been comprehensively explored in an excellent study by Audretsch (1995). He found, for his sample of 11,000 manufacturing businesses set up in 1976,[5] that the likelihood of their survival to 1986 was affected by the following.

1   *MES.* The higher the MES at plant level, the lower the chances of survival. The rationale for this finding is not difficult to find. For any given initial size, the larger the MES, the bigger the cost disadvantage faced by the entrant. MES is not easily measured, but Audretsch (1995) uses a measure widely adopted elsewhere, the mean size of the largest plants in the firm's industry which account for 50 per cent of the output.

   As the earlier discussion on the LRAC function suggests (p. 18), the *shape* of this function is also likely to be an important consideration here (although this is not directly considered by Audretsch). If the function is saucer shaped, then the cost disadvantage faced by a firm that is smaller than MES will be much less than where the function is V shaped.

2   *The start-up size of firm.* For a given MES, the larger the firm's own initial size is, the lower the cost disadvantage it has to overcome, and thus the higher are its chances of survival.

3   *The overall rate of innovation in the firm's industry.* The higher this rate, the greater the uncertainty faced by the entrant, and thus the higher the rate of exit.

4   *The rate of innovation among small firms in the firm's industry.* The argument in (3) applies with even greater force where the technological 'regime' is particularly conducive to innovation by small firms. Winter (1984), drawing on Schumpeter, has distinguished between an 'entrepreneurial' regime which is more favourable to innovation by entrants and less favourable to innovation by established firms, and a 'routinised' regime where the reverse is true. New entry is likely to be higher in the former, but the survival rate is likely to be lower, since relatively more firms will be engaged in innovative activity, with all its attendant uncertainties. In routinised regimes, on the other hand, new entrants are much less likely to enter the industry on the basis of an innovation, and will thus have a lower probability of exit. The particular measure used by Audretsch (1995) was the number of innovations in firms with fewer than 500 employees divided by the total number of employees in such firms. It is not known how sensitive these results are to the particular measure used.

5   *The growth rate of the industry.* Audretsch (1995) argues that the higher this growth rate, the greater the chances of survival. One reason for this is that growth tends to be positively associated with profitability; hence the viability of incumbent firms will be less threatened by entry (and as a result, such firms will be less likely to take retaliatory action). A growing industry will also mean that entrants can come in without taking sales from existing businesses.

6   *Whether the firm is a multi-plant operation.* Where a firm has more than one plant, its *overall* employment size will be a poor measure of the average employment size of its constituent plants. The gap between MES and the size of individual plants will thus *appear* to be less than it really is. It would be expected that, because of this overstatement, a multi-plant firm would be less likely (other things being equal) to survive.

There is one further finding on survival from the Audretsch (1995) study that is worth noting. If the analysis is focused only on those firms which survived to 1984, and on the survival of *this subset of firms* to 1986, the signs of the co-efficients for the overall innovation rate and the small firm innovation rate become positive (for the whole period, 1976–86 they are negative), although only the latter rate is statistically significant. This suggests that new entrants that have survived for the previous eight years are *more* likely to stay in business for the next two, the more innovative the environment. This finding is con-sistent with the proposition that such firms, having found their feet, are more likely to have found an innovation-based market niche for themselves. The sign on MES also changes and ceases to be significant.

These findings highlight the importance of underlying economic influences in determining survival. New entrants ignore these factors at their peril. Audretsch's (1995) study also provides pointers to the appropriate questions that a would-be small business owner might ask prior to setting up. For example, at what size will it be possible to compete in costs terms with rivals? Is the industry, both generally and in relation to small business in particular, a fast moving one technologically and what are the risks associated with entering that environment? How rapidly is the industry growing? How likely is entry to provoke retaliation from incumbent firms who face a potential drop in sales?

The growth of new firms

There are numerous ways in which growth may be measured. Employment, sales, value added, assets and profits are the main options. There may sometimes be a trade-off between the different measures. For example, employment or assets can usually be expanded at the expense of profits. Different measures may rank firms differently, especially where these firms are operating in different sectors. The work reported in this section uses a variety of measures, although employment (which is of particular interest to policymakers) figures most prominently.

Some evidence

It may be helpful at the outset to provide some background evidence for the discussion. Most new businesses do not grow at all. For example Duncan and Handler (1994) suggest that over two-thirds of US new surviving businesses had the same employment nine years after 'birth', defined in their study as the year in which they entered the Dun and Bradstreet (D&B) database. This criterion almost certainly excludes a large number of 'one man bands' which never grow. Hence the Duncan and Handler proportion is likely to be significantly understated.

The D&B database is dominated by businesses in services. It might be expected that the situation in manufacturing might be rather different, given the greater need to achieve economies of scale. In a UK study of a small sample of new manufacturers, Johnson (1986: 86) found that the mean employment size of survivors was just fifteen, six years after birth, a result that tallies closely with that found by Stone (1992: Table 5). It should be noted that this figure relates to survivors only; the average is not weighted by the 'zero' employment of non-survivors.

In Audretsch (1994) US data on the growth profile of those new manu-facturing firms established in 1976 and surviving to 1986 are provided. The mean size of these survivors – nearly eight employees in 1976 – had grown to only twenty-one employees over the ten-year period, although not surprisingly, the spread of firm size consistently increased over the period: by 1986, the standard deviation was thirty-seven employees compared with twelve employees in 1976. Audretsch's (1994: 14) data does not of course include firms whose records do not provide employment data.[6] Almost certainly, these excluded firms will be the smallest ones. The reported average start-up size of the firms included may thus be somewhat biased upwards. In all these studies, the definition of 'birth' is crucial to the interpretation of the results.

So far only the average growth profiles of new firms have been discussed. A tiny minority of firms may however experience very rapid growth. The term 'gazelles' has been used by David Birch to describe such businesses.[7] Not all such businesses are small, though many are. Furthermore, a sizeable minority of gazelles are not young; Birch calculates that about one-fifth have been in operation for thirty years or more. Interestingly, it is by no means the case that all gazelles are located in the high tech sectors. Indeed only one in fifty may be regarded as being in truly high tech industries (*Inc Magazine*, May 1996).

Given the high exit rate in the early years, and the fact that, for many surviving firms, growth is either modest or does not occur at all, it is not sur-prising to find that the probability of any given particular new firm reaching a significant size is low. For example, some years ago, Storey (1982: 22–3) estimated that the probability of a new manufacturing business reaching one hundred employees in the East and West Midlands and Cleveland in the United Kingdom within a decade of birth was less than 1 per cent. Some firms do of course make it through to a very substantial size: after all, the current industrial and commercial giants were new at some stage. However even for new businesses that grow to a substantial size, it may take a very long time to challenge existing leaders (see p. 4).

Stages of growth

A number of commentators have suggested that firms go through a sequence of stages (or phases) in their development. Perhaps the most well known 'stage model' is that proposed by Churchill and Lewis (1983) in their important article from the early 1980s. They distinguished five stages through which new firms develop. These stages are as follows.

1   *Existence:* a key preoccupation here is with ensuring basic business viability.
2   *Survival:* the emphasis changes here from 'mere existence' to getting the balance right between revenues and expenses.
3   *Success:* now the business has established itself, the owner has to decide whether to go for growth (*Success – growth*) or to focus on developing a stable business that will enable the owner to disengage from the business to do other things (*Success – Disengagement*).
4   *Take-off:* the challenge here is achieving rapid growth and the financing of that growth.
5   *Resource maturity:* in this stage the central issues are how to 'consolidate and control the financial gains . . . from rapid growth and . . . to retain the advantages of small size, including flexibility of response and the entrepreneurial spirit'.

Churchill and Lewis (1983) allude to the possibility that for some businesses, there might be a sixth stage of 'Ossification', marked by 'a lack of innovative decision-making and the avoidance of risks'. They see each stage as being associated with a distinctive managerial approach and organisational structure and systems, as well as with a different set of strategic goals and ownership involvement. So, for example, in the 'Existence' phase, the owner directly supervises the business, the organisation is very simple, there are few formal systems in place, the primary goal is simply to exist and the owner more or less *is* the business. In the 'Resource Maturity' phase however, all this has changed. Management is decentralised, the organisation is inevitably more complex, formal systems are extensive, and the strategic focus is on the rate of return. The owner and business are now clearly separate entities. Importantly, Churchill and Lewis (1983) take the view that progression may sometimes be reversed. Thus uni-directional movement through the different stages is not inevitable.

The Churchill and Lewis (1983) approach has been built on by others: see for example the rather more comprehensive approach of Scott and Bruce (1987), together with the references these authors provide and the framework more recently suggested in Burns (2007: 218–9).

These stage models have considerable value in describing the phases that many firms may go through in their life cycle and the different challenges that they may have to face in each phase. However, the boundaries of the stages are not particularly well defined and the empirical support for strong generalisations is not strong. Furthermore, the approach does not typically provide a basis either for predicting when or whether a firm will move on to the next stage or revert back to a preceding one, or for identifying what action may be needed to enable a firm to move from one stage to the next.

Intergenerational transfers

There is another sense in which the small firm may go through phases of development which is not captured by the above stages approach but which may nevertheless be of critical significance for survival and growth. It is the effective transition of management and leadership from one generation of family owners to another.

This is a challenge that affects large numbers of small businesses. For example, according to Birley (1986), 98 per cent of US firms are family owned, but only 30 per cent survive into the second generation. About 15 per cent make it into the third generation. In Britain, the respective figures are 24 and 14 per cent and in Australia, about 11 per cent survive to the third generation and 6 per cent to the fourth. (The British and Australian figures are quoted in Department of Trade and Industry 2004b: A11.) Given that the timing and coverage of studies varies, there is a remarkable similarity in these estimates.

It is interesting that the probability of passing on a business *increases* with each generation. For example, in the United Kingdom, while 24 per cent of first generation businesses transfers to the second generation (see above), 50 per cent of second generation businesses transfers to the third and 70 per cent of third generation businesses to the fourth (quoted in Department of Trade and Industry 2004b: A11). One possible explanation suggested by the DTI for this improvement in the transfer 'rate' is that some organisational learning goes on through the generations. This learning in turn makes transition less problematic.

Problems of succession are far from being confined to family-owned businesses, but they are likely to be rather more acute, given the more limited pool of talent that such a business can draw on and given that the social complexities may be rather more intense. It is important to remember here however that a failure to pass on a business within the family does not necessarily mean that the business itself fails. The business may still survive, but under different ownership.

Le Breton-Miller et al. (2004) have looked at the factors making for successful transition in family businesses and identified those that received the most mentions in the empirical and theoretical literature on the topic over the thirty years or so prior to their study. Their results are not surprising. For example, the motivation of both the incumbent and his or her successor and the relationship between them, the career development and training of the successor and succession planning, all figure as important determinants (along with other factors) of the success of the transition.

Two observations may be made on the factors identified in the Le Breton-Miller et al. (2004) study. The first is that only some of the variables can be significantly manipulated – by, for example, policymakers. Allowing some family-owned businesses to fail may sometimes be the most efficient strategy for reallocating productive resources. Second, the factors identified tend to concentrate on those internal to the business (or the family). It would be surprising however if the economic and wider family context within which the business operates did not exercise an important influence on success.

Some determinants of new firm growth

Audretsch's (1995) US study casts some valuable light on the determinants of the growth of surviving start-ups. He argues that the factors affecting the survival rate (see the section on 'Survival' above) also influence the firm's growth, although not always in the same direction.

First, there is some evidence that MES exercises a positive influence on firm growth in the immediate post-birth years. The argument here is that the higher the MES, the more rapidly a young firm needs to grow in order to overcome its cost disadvantage. Second, Audretsch (1995) shows that firm growth in the early years is negatively and significantly affected by start-up size, the argument here being that the larger this size, the *less* cost pressure there is to grow in order to minimise the effects of entry at sub-optimal scale. Not surprisingly however, Audretsch shows that scale economies and initial size lose their significance after a firm has survived for some years. A plausible explanation for this is that by this stage, the firm will have found ways to compensate for any cost disadvantage it may have had.

Third, surviving firms operating in a technological regime in which there is more small firm innovative activity, tend to grow significantly faster, certainly in their early years. Thus although such a regime lowers the survival rate, it nevertheless systematically raises the growth rates of those firms that do survive.

Fourth, and not surprisingly, there is some suggestion from Audretsch's (1995) results that industry growth exercises a positive effect on surviving firms.

Finally, it is worth noting that the sign on the multi-plant variable is positive in the growth equation, reflecting the fact that the initial size of firm variable is understating the distance that may exist between initial size and *plant* MES and hence the growth that is needed to achieve optimality.

Audretsch's (1995) analysis has very strong intuitive appeal and as with the survival analysis, highlights the important role played by economic factors in determining the growth of young firms. However, it should be noted that the amount of variation in growth rates that he has been able to explain over the whole period 1976–86 is still less than 20 per cent. This suggests that there is a range of other factors that is likely to be important in explaining new firm growth. Some additional factors are suggested below.

Motivation

Business founders differ in their *desire* to grow and this fact, in turn, is likely (other things being equal) to lead to variations in actual growth experience. As Penrose (1980) has pointed out in her seminal book on firm growth: 'a good businessman need not be a particularly ambitious one, and so long as a firm is dominated by men who are not ambitious always to make profits it is unlikely that the firm will grow very large' (Penrose 1980: 35).

A number of studies have examined growth objectives and motivations among SMEs. For example, Hakim (1989) looked at the growth aspirations of independent firms of under fifty workers. She found that only about 10 per cent of firms (out of nearly three-quarters of a million surveyed) were planning fast growth, while 55 per cent had no plans for growth.

Now the precise figures cannot be taken too seriously. As Hakim (1989) pointed out, small changes of emphasis in the wording of questions in surveys can significantly affect the response. However she also presented other survey evidence that supports the conclusion that significant numbers of small firms are not orientated towards growth. This finding is consistent with studies that have developed typologies of small firm owners,[8] and shown that a substantial proportion of owner managers may be content with their current scale of operations. Owners of 'lifestyle' or 'craft' businesses, for example, do not typically have an interest in growing to any significant scale. Hakim's (1989) findings are also consistent with a number of more recent studies which point to relatively low growth aspirations among 'nascent entrepreneurs' in a number of countries, including the United States, Sweden and Denmark (see the summary in Davidsson 2005: 31).

Not all the evidence points so clearly to the conclusion suggested by Hakim (1989). For example, Barkham (1992) looked at growth motivations among recently formed independent business in three UK regions: the South East, the North East and the West Midlands. He found that in these regions, the percentage of these businesses reporting 'medium' or 'high' growth motivation were 90, 80 and 74 per cent respectively. (It is worth noting in passing that the percentage was highest in the South East, the most vibrant region in economic terms.) Again, a study by Cosh and Hughes (2000a: 39) found that about 70 per cent of their 1999 SME sample intended to grow 'moderately or 'substantially' over the following three years. (This survey was a follow-up to firms originally approached in 1997).

It is a little difficult to identify precisely why these later studies suggest a different picture to that painted by Hakim (1989). A significant part of the explanation is likely to be in the samples used. In the Barkham (1992) study, for example, the fact that the firms were all recent formations may have affected the results: new firms may have more energy and opportunity to grow than the general run of established small businesses. And it should be noted that Cosh and Hughes' (2000a) survey was a follow-up to a previous one; this may have had an impact on the findings, with some of the less successful firms leaving the cohort in the intervening period. In all the studies, the terms used are rather loose; this in turn makes comparability across surveys difficult. At the same time it is interesting to note that the Cosh and Hughes study reports that growth aspirations are lowest among the smallest size bands, i.e. those that dominate the Hakim data set.

Whatever the precise picture on motivation, it should be emphasised that *aspiration* to grow may not always translate into *actual* growth. Cosh and Hughes (2000a: 40) show that of those SMEs wanting to grow 'moderately' or 'significantly' in their 1997 survey, 42 per cent in the event remained static or declined. The *ability* and *opportunity* to grow are key factors here (Morrison et al. 2003).

Characteristics of the owner

Audretsch (1995) does not incorporate any variables which directly reflect the human capital possessed by the owner. Yet given the relative smallness of the businesses, the abilities of the owners will have an important influence on the progress of the business. Owners have at least three types of capital. The first may be described as their social capital. This captures their networks and contacts, which in turn affect their ability to obtain supplies and services and to develop their markets. Second, there is their human capital. This consists of the management and financial skills, experience and abilities that owners bring to their businesses, including the capacity to develop appropriate business strategies. Attention has already been drawn above to the potential importance of differences in motivation as an explanation of variations in firm growth. The level of education may also exert some influence although empirical findings on this topic are somewhat mixed (for an excellent summary of results up to the early 1990s, see Storey 1994: 127). A number of studies have found a positive and significant effect, but this is not a universal finding. In Johnson et al. (1999), there is a hint of a negative effect – some owners may perceive themselves *over*qualified for some forms of own account activity, and this in turn may lead to frustration which is inimical to growth – but such a finding is unusual. Experience may be captured by a range of variables, such as age (which is likely to reflect general experience), and the level of 'own account' experience. Again, no strong results have been generated by empirical studies.

Then finally, there is the financial capital that owners possess or to which they have access. It has already been shown (p. 42) that personal assets may have an important role to play in setting up; the same is also likely to be true in subsequent growth. Finance for small firms is further considered in Chapter 8.

The market environment

Audretsch's (1995) study picks up a number of relevant aspects of the market environment in which the firm finds itself. However there are other aspects of this environment that may affect the new firm's survival and growth. For example, what is the competitive structure of the market? Is it dominated by a few large firms with high entry barriers, or is it relatively competitive and easy to enter? Is it subject to volatile movements or is it relatively stable? All these factors are likely to influence the growth path of the young firm.

The policy environment

This environment has two important components as far as new firms are concerned. The first relates to general macroeconomic conditions. The importance of these conditions in stimulating formation activity has already been considered (see p. 62). The general regulatory framework might be included here. The second is the particular portfolio of policy measures in operation and the way in which they may have a differential impact on firms of different sizes. Chapter 9 provides a detailed discussion of the issues.

Size, age and growth

The discussion in the previous section focused primarily on the growth of new firms. In this section, the more general issue of how the size and age of small firms are related to their growth is considered. Two key questions are addressed here. First, do small firms tend to grow faster than their larger counterparts? Second, do younger firms grow more quickly than older firms?

The Law of Proportionate Effect

What is known about the relationship between size and growth? A good starting point for a discussion on this relationship is the Law of Proportionate Effect (LPE), sometimes known as Gibrat's Law (Gibrat 1931). LPE postulates that firm growth is a stochastic phenomenon. Of course it is not difficult to suggest specific features of small-scale operations that either inhibit or facilitate growth. Growth-*inhibiting* factors may include, for example, poorer access to funds; fewer opportunities to exploit economies of scale; and a motivation that may not rank growth very highly. Growth-*facilitating* characteristics may be the greater flexibility of small firms; their bigger incentive to get to a size where they *can* compete effectively; an owner's stronger personal identification with the success of the business; and a higher commitment to personalised service, a particularly important requirement for growth in some industries, notably services.

On top of these factors, a range of external influences may impact differentially on firms of different sizes. These influences may include policy shifts, changes in market conditions and macroeconomic 'shocks'. The underlying assumption of LPE is that the overall impact of all these different forces is that *together* they operate to produce a random effect on firm growth. Thus there is no particular size of firm that is conducive to growth.

Three implications of LPE should be noted: firms in different size bands will have the same mean proportionate growth rate; the *dispersion* of growth rates around this mean will be the same in each size band; and growth rates in any given period will be independent of the growth rate in the previous period.

LPE: the evidence

A vast number of studies aimed at testing the empirical validity of this law have been undertaken (for a good summary up to the early 1990s, see Dunne and Hughes 1994). The majority of these studies have used databases which are mostly made up of firms towards the top of the size distribution. However there are some studies that cover firms across a wider size spectrum or which focus exclusively on small firms. It is these studies that are the focus here.

One of the most comprehensive UK studies is that by Dunne and Hughes (1994) who based their analysis for 1975–85 – and two five-year sub-periods – on all independent companies in the financial and non- financial sectors which were on the *Extel* database, i.e. all quoted and the larger unquoted companies. Although their study covers a wider range of firm sizes than most other comparable studies, it still suffers from severe under-representation of very small businesses, most of which are not incorporated (see p. 102). Around 25 per cent of their sample employed fewer than 500 people, whereas the percentage for the United Kingdom business population in this size category, including those firms with no employees, is well over 99 per cent.[9] Nevertheless a number of their results are of interest.

First, their summary of results of published studies highlights the possibility that the size–growth relationship may have changed over time, with the advantage in growth terms moving from larger firms in the 1950s to smaller ones in the 1960s and 1970s. This suggests, importantly, that some empirical results may be time specific. Policy changes may have something to do with the shift Dunne and Hughes identified: in the 1950s there was much more emphasis on assisting larger firms, whereas in the 1970s and onwards the policy focus switched to smaller firms.

Second, their study, which measures size (and growth) in net assets terms, suggested that overall, small firms tend to grow faster. There is however a suggestion of a threshold effect; beyond this threshold size,[10] the mean growth of firms in different size bands is fairly stable. Dunne and Hughes show that in broad terms, the small firm's advantage in growth terms still holds when they disaggregate the data over nineteen industries. Thus industry effects are not accounting for the results. Their findings are supported in a comprehensive study of US manufacturing over the period 1976–80 (Evans 1987). (Employment was used as the growth metric in this study.) For further evidence see also the review in Scherer and Ross (1990: 141–6).

Third, they found an inverse relationship between size and the variance of growth rates. This finding may in part be explained by the fact that in the smaller firm categories, there is a greater preponderance of younger, inexperienced management. Another possible explanation is that larger firms tend to be more diversified and are thus able to spread their risk across sectors and projects. This finding on the variance of growth is not universally found although the weight of evidence (Scherer and Ross 1990: 144–5) supports Dunne and Hughes.

Finally, Dunne and Hughes (1994) found that for those firms that survived both sub-periods, there is only very limited support for the hypothesis that growth in the second period was significantly influenced by growth in the first period.

The relationship between *age* and growth may now be briefly explored. In their study, Dunne and Hughes (1994) found fairly strong evidence that the age of firms is negatively related to growth. Thus the older the firm, the slower its growth tends to be. This suggests a life cycle effect at work. Again, these results are supported by Evans' (1987) US study of manufacturing firms.

Although Dunne and Hughes covered a wider size spectrum than many previous studies of the relationship between size and growth, firms at the smaller end of the size spectrum were inevitably underrepresented. Dobson and Gerrard's (1989) very small-scale study of the Leeds engineering sector which covered seventy-nine firms mostly within the eleven to fifty employee size band provides some useful supplementary evidence on smaller firms. They found a negative though not statistically significant effect of size on growth in the early 1980s, where size and growth are measured by real sales and real assets. Dobson and Gerrard argue that this result reflects the fact that larger firms have 'already exploited their best opportunities for growth' – although they provide no direct evidence on this score – and that a given proportionate increase in size requires increasingly greater absolute increases. The latter is of course true by definition, but it is unclear precisely why this should impede growth, if a larger absolute size also provides a better *basis* for firm growth (e.g. through the provision of specialist management).

These authors also found that the age of the business had a significant positive effect on the growth of both sales and assets. They argue that older firms 'will be more able to pursue their preferred objective of higher growth'. They do not spell out *why* this might be the case, but the hypothesis does fit in quite nicely with notions of managerial learning. This result on age is in contrast to that found by Dunne and Hughes (1994) but it may be explained by the fact that the Leeds study focuses on relatively young firms. There may well be a positive effect of age in early years, and then a negative effect. In his study of small firms in Scotland – 78 per cent had ten or fewer employees – in the 1980s, Reid (1993: 198f) found that when he regressed growth on size, and business age (with all variables being measured in terms either of sales or assets), size had a significant negative effect, and age was negative but insignificant. However it should be noted that when Reid introduced other more 'thoroughgoing economic variables' – relating to the nature of the market and its competitive characteristics – into his equations (Reid 1993: 201–2), size ceased to be significant, though still remaining negative. Age remained negative but insignificant.

Review

The kind of study undertaken by the investigators mentioned above is not without methodological challenges. The possibility of sample bias has already been mentioned. But another problem arises from what may be called *sample attrition*. This problem reflects the possibility that small, slow growing firms may be more likely to fail than large, slow growing firms. If this is the case, then an analysis of growth that is concerned with survivors alone will be biased towards finding an inverse relationship between size and growth. The argument here is that the poor growth large firms will simply slide down the size distribution for a considerable period before dying, rather than go out of business, whereas the small firm with a similar growth record is more likely to be forced to exit – to hit the buffers earlier. Thus studies of the size–growth relationship may be biased toward finding that in the smaller size bands, growth of *survivors* is faster than in the larger size bands because the slow or negative growers have been weeded out by death. Dunne and Hughes (1994) provide some evidence to support the notion that slow growing small firms are more likely to die than fast growing ones. Thus one has to be careful about attrition bias, although their study also shows that their basic results are unaffected.

It seems fairly clear from these studies that as far as SMEs are concerned, there is little empirical support for the LPE. If anything, the larger the SME, the lower its growth tends to be. As Audretsch (2002) shows, this result is supported by research in numerous countries, although as he also points out, there are a few studies that show different results. The variance of growth also appears to fall with size band. The effect of age is rather more ambiguous, reflecting the fact that as a business ages, both growth reducing factors (e.g. ossification; loss of energy on the part of owners; fewer market opportunities) and growth enhancing factors (e.g. greater maturity; better familiarity with relevant markets) are at work.

Barriers to growth

Much has been written over the years about the barriers to growth that small businesses face. Surveys of the problems and obstacles encountered by small business have become fairly commonplace. In these surveys, respondents are either asked to volunteer details on the key barriers they face, or are asked to evaluate the significance of specific potential barriers that are put to them. Table 6.1 provides a good example of this kind of survey. It is based on a careful analysis of the survey responses of well over 8000 SMEs in the United Kingdom in 2003 (Atkinson and Hurstfield 2004). It combines both prompted and invited responses. In the first five columns of data, percentages relating to the mention of different obstacles are provided, with the data broken down by size category. In the last two columns the *greatest* obstacle for the sample as a whole are identified. It should be noted that the responses relate to obstacles to *success*, rather than growth. Businesses may not evaluate the former in terms of the latter.

Table 6.1 Obstacles to the success of SME businesses

% who said	Obstacles					Greatest obstacle	
	All (%)	No. of employees (%)	Micro (%)	Small (%)	Medium (%)	All (%)	No. of employees (%)
The economy	40.8	37.2	46.8	53.3	56.8	12.0	11.8
Obtaining finance	12.3	10.9	15.5	15.1	16.2	3.3	3.2
Cash flow	31.5	30.0	35.2	34.6	32.1	9.9	9.9
Taxation	38.1	34.4	45.6	50.4	45.9	9.4	9.1
Recruiting staff	21.1	14.9	31.6	51.1	60.4	6.4	4.5
Keeping staff	7.8	4.7	13.3	21.1	31.8	0.7	0.6
Transport issues	15.3	13.5	18.5	23.8	30.9	3.1	3.3
Lack of broadband access	8.0	8.1	7.9	8.2	8.7	1.2	1.5
Regulations	38.7	34.8	44.6	60.7	69.2	14.5	14.1
Keeping up with new technology	15.9	16.4	14.6	16.3	15.6	1.8	2.4
Availability/cost of premises	19.4	18.1	22.3	22.2	23.1	4.1	4.4
Competition	39.2	35.1	47.1	53.6	61.8	16.2	16.0
Shortage of managerial skills/expertise	12.0	9.9	15.1	23.3	32.1	1.6	1.4
No obstacles	9.7	11.7	5.9	2.0	0.4	na	na
Other	na	na	na	na	na	9.6	11.0
No opinion	—	—	—	—	0.2	5.9	6.7
Unwilling to answer	—	—	—	0.1	—	0.3	0.2

Source: Adapted from Atkinson and Hurstfield (2004: Tables 5.1a and 5.2a). Crown copyright: reproduced under the terms of the Click-Use Licence.

Table 6.1 uses 'mentions' as the basis for its data. These figures are not weighted by importance. Other surveys (e.g. Cosh and Hughes 2000a) provide respondents with a scale of potential responses, thereby allowing for the weighting of responses. Nevertheless the kind of information contained in Table 6.1 can be useful in helping to identify perceived impediments to growth and the views of businessmen and women about their relative importance. It can be especially useful when used to track changes in responses over time. It can also be helpful in identifying differences across types of SMEs.

It is clear from the first column that issues over 'The economy', 'Taxation', 'Regulations' and 'Competition' are widely perceived as barriers to success, with the last two being identified as the greatest obstacles (sixth column of data). The marked variations in mentions across size categories is also noticeable. For example, 'The economy', 'Recruiting staff', 'Keeping staff', 'Regulations', 'Competition' and 'Shortage of managerial skills/expertise' all show a higher proportion of mentions as the size band increases.

Data of the kind presented in Table 6.1 present challenges over interpretation. For example, what precisely do respondents have in mind when they say 'The economy' is an obstacle to success? Is this response simply another way of expressing a general wish that the economic environment should be more favourable to a particular business, something that *all* businesses presumably would value? Again, is the identification of 'Taxation' as a problem anything more than an expression that respondents would like its level – and the associated regulations – to be more favourable to business? The survey on which Table 6.1 is based does provide more detailed analyses of the responses which in turn provide useful pointers to what in particular the respondents have in mind, but it is still difficult to interpret the results in a clear way. There is also the issue of potential response bias. Are the responses influenced significantly by a desire on the part of respondents to influence particular aspects of policy? Finally it should be noted that Table 6.1 does not permit an assessment of whether the obstacles identified are *distinctive* to SMEs.

Interpretation of the results would be greatly aided by an empirical analysis of the relationship between the sort of responses reported in Table 6.1 and firm growth. This would help to provide a clearer evidence base on how owners perceptions of barriers translate into actual business development.

Concluding comment

This chapter has been able to identify a number of factors that affect the survival and growth of new firms. It has also looked specifically at the effects of firm size and age on growth. It is clear however that much remains unexplained, a reflection of the complex array of factors that influence the development of small and new firms. It is also likely these factors change over time. Indeed, it might well be argued that it is precisely the ability of firms to identify and harness new influences, to buck trends, that is likely to be a major contributor to growth over the longer term.

Surveys of the obstacles to small business success provide some useful insights into the perceptions of small business owners and managers, but great care must be taken in deriving policy implications from their results.

7 The economic role of small firms

Introduction

In this chapter, a number of facets of the economic contribution made by small firms is examined. This contribution – and how it might be enhanced – is often seen as critically important by policymakers concerned with improving economic performance. This is apparent in the United Kingdom for example, where the government expressed its view in 2002 as follows.

> For much of the twentieth century, economic forces and government policies gave priority to large-scale production. Small business was seen to be inefficient or unimportant in promoting economic growth and prosperity. But since the 1970s, the small business sector has experienced a marked resurgence. Today, small businesses and the entrepreneurial spirit that drives them lie at the heart of the Government's strategy to improve economic performance, by boosting productivity and increasing opportunity and prosperity throughout the UK.
>
> (HM Treasury and Small Business Service 2002b: 1)

It is interesting to see how small business and the 'entrepreneurial spirit' are so closely linked both in this extract and in the source document as a whole. A similarly strong linkage is apparent in the document between small business and the 'enterprise economy'. The possible limitations of such an approach have already been highlighted (see p. 28).

There are many aspects of the economic contribution made by small firms. In this chapter, four areas are considered: employment, innovation, competition and economic growth.

Employment

The broader picture

Much has been written and spoken in recent years about employment creation in small firms. David Birch's (1979) early work in the United States provided a major stimulus for research and policy interest in this topic. His initial finding, based on a data file of 5.6 million establishments, was that small firms, defined as those with twenty or fewer employees, accounted for 66 per cent of all *net* new jobs generated in the United States over the period 1969 to 1976. (Total net new jobs is defined here as the total number of jobs in 1976 less the total number in 1969; the term 'jobs', employed here and elsewhere in this chapter, is used synonymously with 'employment'.) Although the methodology underlying Birch's (1979) study and his results were subsequently criticised – see for example Armington and Odle (1982) and Davis et al. (1996) – his research was published at a time of increasing unemployment throughout the western world. It therefore found a receptive audience among policymakers and academics. As a result, numerous studies on employment creation in small firms were published during the 1980s and 1990s.

A useful starting point is to look at what has been happening to the share of small firms in total employment over time. Such exercises carry a number of dangers. Statistical definitions change over time and the collection of data on very small firms is problematic. Estimation is often involved. Part-time employment is sometimes given the same weight as full-time employment. Furthermore the headcount figures take no account of the 'quality' of the jobs in terms of characteristics such as working conditions, remuneration, job security or safety. Aggregation over industries and/or countries carries obvious dangers. These limitations need to be borne in mind in the following discussion.

The behaviour over time of the share of small firm employment in advanced economies has been subject to much debate. Loveman and Sengenberger (1991) have argued from their data covering the United States, Japan, France, Germany, the United Kingdom and Italy, that the share of both small enterprises and a small establishments fell through the late 1960s and early 1970s and then increased into the 1980s. (Johnson 1978 has shown that in UK manufacturing, the preceding decline was a long-term one, stretching back to at least the 1930s.) Loveman and Sengenberger (1991) comment as follows on their data:

> What is remarkable about this finding is not that the recent growth in small unit employment has been enormous in all countries, but rather that the pattern of decline and then growth is so robust over such a wide sample of countries, sectors, size distributions, and institutions.
>
> (Loveman and Sengenberger 1991: 7)

Audretsch (2002) provides further supporting evidence for the turn round in the relative importance of small firms in the United States and most European countries in the mid-1970s. Storey (1994: 28–31) has however argued that the Loveman and Sengenberger (1991) data reveal a rather more complex picture; indeed, he argues that it is only in the United Kingdom that the U shape is clear. Data on the share of self-employment in total employment (see p. 14) confirm the diversity of experience across countries.

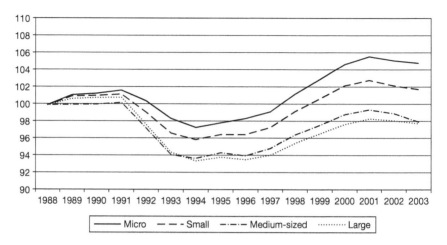

Figure 7.1 Employment trends by employment size of businesses, Europe-19

Source: See European Commission (2004: 36). Estimated by EIM Business Policy & Research; estimates based on Eurostat's Structural Business Statistics and Eurostat's SME Database; also based on *European Economy* Supplement A, May 2003, and *OECD Economic Outlook*, no. 71, June 2003

More recent experience for Europe as a whole is captured in Figure 7.1, which looks at the employment of (non-primary, private) enterprises of different sizes in the Europe-19 countries over the period 1988–2003. Figure 7.1 should be examined in the light of the limitations outlined earlier, although it is unlikely that these would affect the general picture that emerges from the graph. The implication of the data in the graph is that overall, both micro and small businesses increased their *share* of employment over the period. The recession in the early 1990s affected all four categories although the micro and small businesses were more resilient. How far the overall trends have reflected the growing importance of sectors where micro and small firms are relatively more important and how far they have reflected an increasing share of such firms in given sectors (see the analysis on pp. 14–16) is unclear.

Differences in experience across economic regions are highlighted in Table 7.1 where the Europe-19 and US records are compared for two sub-periods. It is striking that while in Europe, overall employment growth appears (broadly) to be inversely related to size, the opposite is true in the United States. Disaggregation of the European data would almost certainly reveal important inter-country differences. It is also important to note that experience can vary significantly over time: see for example the growth experienced by micro firms in both the European Union and the United States in the two periods. While European micro firms significantly increased their annual overall growth rate in the second period, their counterparts in the United States experienced a considerable reduction in this rate. Such differences are in line with the wide variation in trends in the self-employment rate across countries (Parker and Robson 2004).

Table 7.1 Employment growth by employment size class, Europe-19 and USA, 1993–98 and 1998–2001

	1993–98		1998–2001	
	Europe-19	USA	Europe-19	USA
SMEs	Average annual % change in			
Micro	0.6	1.1	1.4	0.3
Small	0.4	1.9	1.2	1.9
Medium-sized	0.3	2.2	1.0	2.5
Total	0.5	1.8	1.3	1.7
Large-scale enterprises	0.3	3.5	1.0	3.5
All enterprises	0.4	2.7	1.2	2.7

Source: See European Union (2004: 36). Estimated by EIM Business Policy & Research; estimates based on Eurostat's Structural Business Statistics and Eurostat's SME Database; also based on *European Economy*, Supplement A, May 2003, and *OECD Economic Outlook*, no. 71, June 2003. US data are derived from SBA/Census data.

Job accounting

The picture presented in Figure 7.1 and Table 7.1 is the net product of job losses and gains of firms of different sizes. These flows may be captured through a job accounting framework, an approach which was given a substantial boost by Birch (1979). Job accounts break down employment (or job) change in any given period into the following components.

I *Gross employment gains* from
 • IA *Expansions:* this gain is measured by the increase in employment between the base and end years in those firms which were in existence throughout the period, and whose employment was higher in the end year than in the base year.
 • IB *Births:* this gain is measured by the end year employment in those firms which were born during the period, and which were still in existence in the end year.

II *Gross employment losses* from
 • IIA *Contractions:* this loss is measured by the decrease in employment between the base and end years in those firms which were existence throughout the period, and whose employment was lower in the end year than in the base year.
 • IIB *Deaths:* this loss is measured by the base year employment in those firms which died during the period.

The difference between the gross employment gains and losses is the *net employment change.*

In numerous studies, this exercise has been undertaken for different firm size bands. In this way it is possible to look in more detail at the 'mechanics' of employment change. Some researchers have sought to draw conclusions from job accounting data on the relative contribution of different sized firms to overall employment change, and on the variation across size bands in the relative importance of the different components of change outlined above. These issues, which are at the heart of the 'job creation' literature, are considered later in this section. Here the focus is simply on the flows identified in job accounts.

It should be noted that only the base and end years (or dates) are compared when classifying firms which remain in existence throughout the period as 'expanders' or 'contractors'. Thus, for example, a firm that grows after the base year, but then subsequently contracts so that its end year employment is lower than its base year employment will be classified as contracting, even though in terms of person years, it may have provided substantially increased employment over the period.

Table 7.2 provides some illustrative job accounts data for the United States for six size bands for 2002–3 (as the note to the table shows, the data excludes those firms without employees, an important omission). The first three columns of data provide details of the employment and net employment change in each size band. The next four columns break the net employment change into the four job accounting components for each size band, with each component expressed as a percentage of the size band's 2002 employment. The 'turbulence' measure in the last column is defined here as the sum of all four components, ignoring the sign.

Some job accounting data for the United Kingdom for the period 1995–9 are provided in Table 7.3. These data, which are based on Dale and Morgan (2001) and also exclude firms without employees, are not directly comparable with those given in Table 7.2. For example, the size bands are different, and the employment from births is separately identified and is not allocated across size bands. (However, Dale and Morgan (2001) estimate that about 85 per cent of the 2.3 million employed in newly formed firms was in firms of up to 249 employees.) The data also group contractions and deaths together and cover a longer period. They nevertheless provide some useful insights into job accounts for the United Kingdom.

Turbulence

One of the striking features of both Tables 7.2 and 7.3 is the substantial amount of turbulence in the labour market, even over very short periods. For example, Table 7.2 shows that in the United States, overall gross employment gains and losses in 2002–3 were equivalent to 32 per cent of the 2002 employment level. This churning is highest (by a significant margin) in the 1–4 size category, and then declines through the size bands. However even with the largest firms (500+ employees), it is still nearly 30 per cent. A key contributor to the much higher level of turbulence in the smallest size category is the relatively higher

Table 7.2 Job accounts: components of employment change by size of enterprise, USA, 2002–3[a]

Employment size of enterprise in 2002	Employment in 2002 (000s)	Net employment change 2002–3		% change in employment from				Turbulence
		(000s)	As % of 2002 employment	Births	Expansions	Deaths	Contractions	
1–4	5,691.2	1,107.0	19.5	14.8	25.5	–12.6	–8.2	61.2
5–9	6,634.1	307.7	4.6	7.8	14.6	–6.7	–11.1	40.2
10–19	8,241.4	158.8	1.9	6.0	12.4	–5.4	–11.0	34.8
20–99	19,868.7	304.1	1.5	4.4	11.5	–4.1	–10.2	30.2
100–499	15,907.3	112.7	0.7	2.8	12.1	–2.8	–11.3	29.0
500+	56,033.8	–994.7	–1.8	0.9	12.6	–0.8	–14.4	28.6
Total	112,376.7	995.6	0.9	3.3	13.1	–3.0	–12.5	31.9

Source: Derived from data supplied to the Office of Advocacy, US Small Business Administration by the US Census Bureau, Statistics of US Business.

Note: [a] The Census of Business considers the figures in this table to be estimates only. The data exclude farms and businesses without employees. New firms are classified by their end of year size. The year runs from March.

Table 7.3 Job accounting in the United Kingdom, 1995–9[a]

	Births/expansions 1995–9		Deaths/contractions 1995–9		Net employment change 1995–9	
	Employment gains (m)	As % of 1995 employment	Employment losses (m)	As a % of 1995 employment	Employment (m)	As % of 1995 employment
Births[b]	2.3	na	na	na	2.3	na
1–9	0.9	25	−1.3	−37	−0.4	−12
10–49	0.5	16	−1.2	−36	−0.7	−20
50–249	0.5	19	−0.8	−30	−0.3	−11
250+	1.6	16	−1.7	−17	−0.1	−1
Total employment gains/losses	5.8	30	−5.1	−26	0.7	4

Source: Estimated from Dale and Morgan (2001)

Notes: [a] The figures in the table are all subject to rounding error. Data on employment gains and on net employment change for the individual size bands exclude births.
         [b] Firms existing in 1999 but not in 1995.

employment flows associated with births and deaths (employment from expansions is also relatively much higher).

A further point to note from Table 7.2 is that across all size bands, the percentage net employment change is only a fraction of the turbulence figure. Thus even over only one year, a relatively modest overall change in employment is accompanied by a very substantial churning in the labour market. The fraction is at its highest in the smallest band, where it is it is just under one-third (19.5 per cent divided by 61.2 per cent). In the other size bands the fraction is substantially less.

Table 7.3 shows that as in the United States, turbulence in the United Kingdom is very significant relative to the amount of net employment gains. The way in which the data are presented in Table 7.3 makes direct comparison with the United States difficult, but some estimates of turbulence in terms of levels of employment involved can be provided. The net employment change overall is 0.7 million, whereas turbulence is 10.9 million (gross employment gains of 5.8 million plus gross employment losses of 5.1 million). If only firms in the 1–249 size category are considered, then turbulence is around 7.2 million and is associated with a net employment change of about 0.6 million. (In this calculation, the turbulence figure includes 85 per cent of the 2.3 million jobs attributable to births in all size categories.) These figures imply that in firms of 250 or over, net employment change (about 0.2 million) is a much smaller proportion of turbulence (about 3.6 million).

The contribution of small firms to job generation

Job accounting has frequently been used to argue that the smaller firm plays a disproportionate part in the creation of jobs. Table 7.2 provides some basis for this argument, at least in the United States. It shows that the smallest size category of enterprise (1–4 employees) had by far and away the largest (positive) net employment change in percentage terms. The next size band, 5–9 employees, had the second highest percentage. This change was however negative in the 500+ category. The table also shows that without the contribution made by births, net employment change would have been negative in all but the smallest size band. It is worth noting too that the net loss of employment in the largest firms (994,700) was more than offset by the net gain (of 1,107,000) in the smallest firms.

Table 7.3 provides further fragments of evidence from the United Kingdom on the importance of small firms in employment terms. It shows that as in the United States, it is only the contribution of births that keeps the overall net employment change positive. The calculations in the previous section also show that firms of 1–249 employees accounted for most of the overall net employment change of 0.7 million.

Earlier, more detailed work on the United Kingdom was undertaken by Daly et al. (1991) for the period 1987–9. They found that net employment change, as a percentage of the base year employment, was greatest, by a very significant margin, in the 1–4 employees band. However these authors also found that this percentage was higher in firms of 500–999 employees than it was in firms of 5–9, 10–19, 20–49, 50–99 and 100–499 employees, a result suggesting a more complex relationship between size and employment generation than is sometimes assumed. Interestingly, Daly et al. (1991) also show that 55 per cent of *all* net employment came in the 1–19 size category, not so far off the 66 percent suggested by Birch (1979: see above).

Some issues

Notwithstanding this evidence, care must be exercised in reaching a conclusion over the contribution of SMEs to job creation. There are a number of issues to be considered here. First, different time periods and countries may yield very different results. Economic context is important. Second, there are issues surrounding the measurement of jobs. It is not for example always clear whether a simple headcount or a 'full-time equivalents' basis is being used.

Third – and this is relevant where the relative contribution of different size bands is being considered – how firms are classified to a size band may affect the results (Okolie 2004). Such classification may be on the basis of opening, closing or some intermediate size. If it is assumed that there is some long run constant size to which firms tend, then firms may be 'large' ('small') relative to this size because of some transitory increase (decrease) in size in the previous period. Thus it would be expected that on average, large (small) firms will decline (grow) in the period under study as they revert back to their long run size. The possible effects of this 'regression fallacy' have been illustrated by Davis et al. (1996) who use a longitudinal data set on plants in US manufacturing over the period 1972 to 1988 to show how empirical results on job dynamics may change when alternative classification criteria are used. Using a base year classification, the net job change rate falls steeply over the first size bands, and then levels out. However, when end year size is used to classify plants, a positive relationship between plant size and the net job change rate emerges.[1] If the average size over the period is used, no relationship is evident.

The key question of course is how far the assumption behind the regression fallacy is valid. Carree and Klomp (1996) point out that if persistent growth or decline of firms is a possibility, then any correction for the regression fallacy is inappropriate. They argue that the notion of long run size is inappropriate in a world where environmental change is constantly altering the opportunities for growth. These authors suggest that what is needed is an exercise that seeks to separate out any transitory growth from permanent growth and then to examine the permanent component only.

Fourth, any analysis by size band may be sensitive to the precise bands used.

Fifth, even if all above issues are discounted, there is still the fundamental problem of what the figures *mean*. Terms such as job 'creation' and 'generation' are very widely used in association with components of change analysis: see for example Daly et al. (1991). Now in that the employment plainly *occurs* in different categories of firm, the usage of these terms makes sense. However such usage is more questionable where the concern is with identifying the *causes* of employment change. There are at least three questions that need to be addressed here.

- *What is the relationship between the jobs included in the accounting exercise and their effects on employment in the economy as a whole?* If jobs in certain size bands are better paid, then the multiplier effects will be greater. Pay tends to be higher in larger firms (see below). Again, jobs in some size bands may be more 'pivotal' in generating positive employment knock-on effects than others. In other words the 'social product', measured in terms of the overall employment impact, may be higher. There is little empirical evidence on this point, although Audretsch (2002) has argued that the potential presence of spill-over effects may represent 'an important qualification' on the results of job generation studies.

- *What is the relationship between different categories of job change?* Contractions in employment and/or deaths may for example lead to new opportunities for expansions and/or births, as for example more market 'space' is created. Alternatively they may lead to *more* contractions and/or deaths through a domino effect in the marketplace. Conversely, births and expansions may have positive or adverse effects on the opportunities for other potential or existing businesses. An example of a positive effect might be where a new firm develops an innovation that enables other firms to start up or develop. A negative effect would be felt where (say) the birth threatens the existence of a competitor. There is no reason to assume that these effects will be the same in all size bands. The reductions in employment may be in different size bands to those in which the initial increases in employment occur. For example, a large firm may offload its non core activities by encouraging some of its employees to set up in business by themselves in order to supply what were previously in-house activities (see Johnson and Rodger 1983 for some examples). In such cases it might be argued, paradoxically, that it is the contraction of the large firm that is 'creating' or 'generating' the new jobs in the small businesses. The job accounting framework does little to capture the dynamic interrelationships between the different components.

- *What are the fundamental economic forces behind employment change?* If, for example, underlying supply conditions change in such a way that production in smaller firms is favoured, more firms will be found in the lower size bands, to take advantage of the new developments. Contractions and/or deaths in larger firms may also occur. In circumstances such as these, it is not especially helpful to identify smallness per se as doing the employment 'creation' or 'generation'.

Finally, there is the issue of the differing characteristics of jobs and whether these characteristics differ across size bands. There is evidence (from both the

United States and the United Kingdom) to show that employees in small firms tend to be less well rewarded, in terms both of wages/salaries and fringe benefits (Storey 1994: 179–86). Brown et al. (1990: 42) review the US evidence on wages and suggest that even after allowing for differences in labour quality, and industrial structure, the size wage-premium cannot be explained by differences in working conditions,[2] or by union avoidance strategies.[3] The evidence must be treated cautiously – for example, the results may be sensitive to the precise dividing line chosen to separate 'small' from 'large',[4] and the size–wage premium may vary across the size spectrum – but at the very least it provides an indication of a size-related wage differential. What is true of wages also appears to be true of fringe benefits. It may also be implied from the survival data (see p. 65) that employment in small firms is less secure.

The upshot of this discussion is that great care must be taken in evaluating the role of small firms in employment creation. The interrelatedness of the economy and the variation in job characteristics make such evaluation problematic. What is clear however is that a very substantial proportion of jobs is to be found in smaller firms; and that new firms are a key channel for new jobs. The health of new and small firms is therefore of vital significance for the economy.

Innovation

Innovation for Schumpeter, whose seminal work in this area (see for example Schumpeter 1939, 1952) is still highly influential, involved market implementation. Schumpeter defined innovation as 'any "doing things differently" in the realm of economic life' (Schumpeter 1939: 84). As Chapter 3 showed, his definition went beyond purely technological innovation. Although the discussion in this section focuses on such developments, many of the issues raised are also directly relevant to their non-technological counterparts.

Scale and innovation: some arguments

How might the size of firm affect its capacity to innovate? There are a number of factors that may favour large firms. There may be economies of scale in the research and development (R&D) process that often leads up to such innovation. Two sources of such economies may be mentioned. First, there may be a 'threshold' level of R&D effort, below which it is simply not possible to sustain a viable programme of activity. The presence of a threshold effect will in turn mean that firms operating on a small scale will suffer a unit R&D cost penalty compared with the larger businesses. Second, there may be economies of scale in the undertaking of R&D activity itself. There may for example be synergies in the interaction between personnel, such that staff have a higher average level of productivity, the more of them there are. The popular notion of 'critical mass' may be interpreted as a quantum jump in such synergies. Another economy of scale may come from the ability to spread the cost of expensive specialist equipment across higher levels of output.

Typically larger organisations also have better access to finance and if they are diversified, they may face a lower overall risk. In assessing the advantages of size in respect to finance and risk bearing, it is important to remember that the costs of technological innovation include not only R&D expenditure, but also launch costs (e.g. marketing) and the investment necessary to set up production facilities. Indeed R&D may only constitute a small proportion of the total innovation outlay. There is the additional challenge that arises from the need to finance the gap between the initiation of a development and the time the innovation becomes revenue earning. This may be several years. Stoneman (1995: 6) for example suggests a mean innovation 'period' of thirteen years.

It is worth pointing out too that the larger organisation with its stronger financial position, may be better placed to defend its patent position. While obtaining a patent is likely to be within the reach of most firms, the legal and other costs of *enforcing* it may be very high. Thus while a small firm may be able to acquire a patent, it may not have the resources to defend it.

Against these advantages of scale is the possibility that bureaucratic procedures may flourish more in larger organisations, thereby inhibiting the flow and implementation of creative ideas. It is interesting to note here that, contrary to the popular and much espoused view of J. K. Galbraith over half a century ago, that most 'cheap and simple' inventions have already been made (1956: 86) – many of the innovations over the past hundred years have had their source in small-scale business or in the activities of individuals working on their own or with a handful of others (Jewkes et al. 1969). New firms, sometimes formed by individuals who could not get their ideas accepted for development by the large company they previously worked for, have proved to be an important vehicle for innovation. In some cases, of course, it may represent an efficient division of labour for the initial creative activity to be undertaken by a small-scale operation with the development of the idea for market – often involving extensive R&D – being done by a large business.

There are other factors that may mean that smaller firms are not disadvantaged in the process of technological innovation. It may be possible to buy in some services involved in the innovation process, e.g. testing, from the marketplace, thereby reducing the disadvantage of small-scale operation. Furthermore, some 'technological regimes' (Winter 1984) may be intrinsically more suited to innovation by smaller businesses than others.

Some evidence on firm size and innovation

Some of the strongest evidence on firm size and innovation – which relates to the second half of the twentieth century – comes from Acs and Audretsch (1988) for the United States and from Pavitt et al. (1987) for the United Kingdom. These authors used different small/large firm boundaries: Acs and Audretsch (1988) used 500 employees as a single small/large dividing line, whereas Pavitt et al. (1987) present results across the size range. Acs and Audretsch (1988) found that firms of 500 employees or fewer were overall less important as a source of innovation than larger firms, but that they accounted for a much higher proportion of technological innovation than their employment share might suggest. Pavitt et al. reported broadly similar results for the United Kingdom in the early 1980s, although in their smallest size category (1–99 employees) the innovation/employment ratio was only 0.63, i.e. firms in this size band were significantly *less* innovative than their employment might suggest. This ratio *exceeded* one for the three largest size categories above 10,000 employees. This variation of innovation/employment ratios across size bands in the United Kingdom data highlights the danger of generalising from just one small/large division. Significantly, Pavitt et al. also found variations *over time* in the ratio in individual size bands; these variations reflect changes in the technological and economic environment within which firms operate.

Both the Acs and Audretsch and Pavitt et al. studies show considerable variations in the large firm and small firm innovation breakdown across sectors. Technological conditions vary from sector to sector and it is a mistake to assume that one size fits all. In some, the small firm may have an advantage; in others a disadvantage. For a good discussion on these issues, see Freeman and Soete (1997: 234–40).

The above discussion on the small firm and large firm distribution of innovative activity should not be taken to imply that most small firms are characterised by innovation. Audretsch (2002: 4) has pointed out: 'Even for a developed country such as the United States, only a very small fraction of new start-ups are really innovative'. The same will be true of the stock of small firms.

So far the focus has been on small firms *that remain in existence*. It is however important to remember that firms that *fail* may also provide an important economic role in signalling innovations –or ways of introducing innovations – that are *not* viable. In this way the overall level of market knowledge is enhanced.

Competition

Despite the massive literature that now exists on small firms, there has been relatively little discussion of the effects of such firms on competition. In this section the role in the competitive process, first, of existing small firms and second, of new firms is considered.

Existing small firms

In most 'sectors' (or 'industries') as defined in official statistics, firms of very different sizes coexist. This may reflect the fact there is no one optimum size for productive activity. No size has an overall cost advantage or disadvantage. In other words the long run average cost function is flat-bottomed. (An important factor here may be the ability of the small firm to buy in services that *do* display production economies of scale and thus to eliminate or reduce the cost advantages that would otherwise be possessed by their larger counterparts.) However there may be more subtle explanations. One possibility is that the 'sector' is in fact a diverse one, covering a number of productive activities where scale is important in some but not in others. 'Retailing' is a good example. While there are very substantial economies to be exploited in (say) the standard kind of food supermarket, this is much less true in highly specialist outlets such as a florist or jewellers where distinctive personalised service is important and for which a large firm would be unsuited.[5] The accommodation market is another good example of a segmented market. The traditional bed and breakfast does not typically compete with large, full-service hotels. Thus small firms may have an important economic role to play in engaging in efficient productive activity in particular market segments. Sometimes there may be a very distinctive market 'niche' that a small firm occupies. This niche may derive from a variety of sources: the firm's location, the highly distinctive service or product it offers, its control of particular supplies, its brand name or customer loyalty. It may have a natural monopoly: there is simply no market 'room' for more than one firm to operate.

In examining the firm size distribution in a sector, it should also be recognised that a snapshot at any given time will not pick up the dynamic process of size adjustment in which many of the firms will be engaged. At any one time, even where a sector is fairly homogenous and where there *is* an optimum size or range, some firms may be seeking to grow to the optimum size while others may have overshot it and be in the process of adjusting their size downwards. Yet others may be in the process of discovering, belatedly for their owners, that they are simply not viable: the evidence presented earlier in this book on early failure (p. 34) and on sub-optimal working (p. 66), suggests that there may be substantial numbers of owners in this category. The picture may be further complicated by the fact that the optimum may itself be shifting as a result of changes in factor prices and or technology. In this context, the growth or decline small firms may provide important information about the whereabouts of the optimum and the size adjustments have to be made.

Whatever the reasons for the coexistence of small and large firms, small businesses may exercise a restraining competitive influence on their larger counterparts' freedom to exploit their market positions. They may introduce productivity or cost advantages that force the larger players to respond. The higher aircraft utilisation of the 'low cost' airlines is a good example. For their part, larger firms may welcome the presence of a 'competitive fringe' as evidence – for the regulatory authorities – that they face strong competitive pressures, provided of course that this 'fringe' does not grow too large. This is particularly likely to be the case where the overall market is growing and the presence of small firms is not a threat to larger firms' existing sales.

Of course there are 'sectors' where economies of scale are exhausted at a very low level. Men's hairdressing is a good example. In these cases, it would be expected that the sector would be populated by small firms and that the level of competition would be high.

The role of new firms

In Chapter 6 the rather obvious point was made that all of today's large businesses were new at some point. And it is still possible for current leaders to be toppled by newcomers that have grown up alongside. In this way the small firms have a 'seedbed' role in competition. It was the possibility of such a challenge that lay behind Alfred Marshall's famous 'trees of the forest' analogy:

> But here we may read a lesson from the young trees of the forest as they struggle upwards through the benumbing shade of their older rivals. Many succumb on the way, and a few only survive; those few become stronger with every year, they get a larger share of light and air with every increase of their height, and at last in their turn they tower above their neighbours, and seem as they would grow on for ever, and for ever become stronger as they grow. But they do not. One tree will last longer in full vigour and attain a greater size than another; but sooner or later age tells on them all. Though the taller ones have a better access to light and air than their rivals, they gradually lose vitality; and one after another they give place to others, which, though of less material strength, have on their side the vigour of youth.
>
> (Marshall 1920: 263)

There are indeed some spectacular cases of long-established large businesses finding themselves severely challenged by newcomers. Again, the impact of the low cost airlines on the established 'majors' is a good example. However it is also important to be cautious about Marshall's analogy. First, Marshall (1920: 263) himself acknowledged that the modern large company might be able to rejuvenate itself. It need not be passive in the face of competitive challenge.[6] Major companies with a long history, who experience a loss of vigour, sometimes prove capable of turning themselves round. Second, the *absolute* level of activity that has to be reached by a newcomer if it is to challenge a leader has grown over time. Thus the task faced by the brand new firm is now greater.

Finally, the evidence suggests that only a very small minority of new businesses ever get to the stage where a substantive challenge is possible. Chapter 6 provided evidence on low survival rates of new businesses and on the small number of survivors who grow to any size. Of those who do grow, only a tiny proportion grow to a size sufficient to topple the market leaders and this will typically take a very long time.

Some fascinating illustrative evidence on market penetration by newcomers is provided by Geroski (1991: 41f) in his study of the UK car industry. Geroski (1991) distinguishes between 'toe-hold' entry, defined as the time when the entrant's cars sold in sufficient numbers to justify a valuation of them for insurance purposes, and 'actual' entry where the entrant's market share reached 1 per cent of the relevant market segment ('small' cars, 'medium' cars and 'large' cars); 1 per cent is hardly a major market share but it does indicate serious entry.

Geroski found that for the twelve entrants he examined, the average lag between toe-hold and actual entry was twenty-six years, with the range being four to forty-three years. All but two of the entrants took at least ten years to make this transition. A number of other toe-hold entrants never became actual entrants. Bearing in mind that Geroski's entrants were all existing firms already in operation in other countries, it is clear that the likelihood of a new, small firm being able to launch an effective challenge in this kind of market is very small indeed. The picture may of course be very different in other industries, particularly where both the technology and market are less mature. Unfortunately, there are no comparable empirical studies available.

The fact that few new firms provide a challenge to existing *leaders* should not detract from the possibility that small-scale formations may nevertheless exercise a strong competitive influence on other small firms. They may force them out of business or to adapt. On the other hand a newcomer may sometimes bolster the competitive viability of existing small businesses through economies of agglomeration. One craft shop located in a tourist centre may not be able to survive. *Several* craft shops may be able to do so, because overall demand may be stimulated by the presence of choice and complementarity.

There is another important economic role for newcomers that is often ignored, but which may play an important part in the competitive process. A formation may be a mechanism for releasing important information on the viability of a business activity that might not otherwise be available. The failure of a new venture may signal *non-* viability, at least without significant improvements in (say) efficiency or demand – in effect revealing that competition is too strong. The success of a venture on the other hand may point to opportunities for other competing ventures.

The above discussion on the competitive effect of newcomers focused on their actual entry. The potential *threat* of entry from a firm that is not already in the market may also have a moderating effect on incumbent firms. In such *contestable* markets (Baumol 1982), the latter firms know that if they act uncompetitively, newcomers will enter and undercut them.

Economic growth

How does the presence of small firms affect economic growth? In the previous sections, various ways in which small firms might contribute positively to measured economic progress were suggested: through innovation, the development of market niches, efficient production, the generation of competitive pressure, the provision of market information and so on. At the same time, it should be recognised that some small firms may, at least for a period, represent *in*efficient productive activity, by for example, operating at sub-optimal scale. And *new* firms may venture into areas that are not viable.

Some investigators have tried to measure the overall impact of small firms on economic growth. For example, using standard regression techniques, Thurik (1999) has tackled the issue by examining the relationship between the share of large enterprises in fourteen manufacturing industries in thirteen European countries and the growth of production in these industries. He used two 'small/large' dividing figures, 100 and 500 employees, and covered the early 1990s. He found 'that a manufacturing industry with a low large firm presence relative to the same industries in other countries . . . performed better in terms of growth of output' (Thurik 1999: 59). This was true for both of the small and large size boundaries used by Thurik.

As Thurik (1991) acknowledges, this kind of exercise is not without its limitations. The results for example, may be period specific. Furthermore, they do not themselves provide insights into *why* they arise.[7] However his study does have the advantage of taking negative and positive influences into account in an overall kind of way. It suggests that the flexibility of smaller firms, their ability to explore new markets and new ways of doing things may be particularly valuable characteristics in the development of a modern economy. Audretsch (1999) provides a good discussion on the relevant issues here.

Further insights into the relationship between small firm activity and economic growth may be gleaned from the 2003 *GEM* study. Reynolds et al. (2004: 19) provide correlations between economic growth and (what is now known as) overall, necessity-based and opportunity-based early-stage entre-preneurial activity (ESEA) (see p. 45) for a range of countries. They found that there was no significant correlation in the current year, but that for all three indexes of ESEA – there was a significant positive correlation with economic growth lagged one year. The correlation with economic growth after a three-year lag was still positive, but was lower than that for a one-year lag for both the overall and opportunity-based ESEA indexes. (It was not statistically significant for the latter.) However for the necessity-based ESEA index, the three-year lag correlation was positive and significant and was much higher than that for the one-year lag.

Now simple correlations can tell only a limited story. But one plausible interpretation of these results is that ESEA does play a part, after a lag, in stimulating economic growth and that necessity-based ESEA has a particularly important role to play here, because it represents a move into productive activity of people who would not otherwise be making any measured economic contribution. The fact that the correlation is highest in year three suggests that it may take some time for 'necessity founders' to become established. It is of course only possible to be very tentative about these conclusions: the underpinning statistical basis inevitably has limitations. It is important too, to stress again that the results may be period specific. In their interesting study of the relationship between (employment) growth and business formation in German regions, Audretsch and Fritsch (2002) found that the experience of the 1980s and the 1990s differed. In the former, no relationship was found; in the latter, business formation exercised a positive effect on growth.

Concluding comment

This chapter has looked at some key aspects of the economic role of small firms. It is clear that any assessment of this role is complex. However while it might be difficult to gauge the precise contribution of small firms, it is evident that, collectively, they play a highly important role in economic progress.

8   Finance

Introduction

The financing of small firms has attracted very extensive interest and debate. This chapter first provides a brief description of the scale of small firms finance and some of its key characteristics. In the next two sections the proposition that there are 'gaps' in small firms financing – a major concern of much of the literature – is explored. The first of these two sections sketches the historical record of investigations into the financing difficulties faced by small firms in the United Kingdom. The second uses some basic supply and demand analysis to tease out a more precise economic meaning for the notion of a finance 'gap'. The final section of the chapter briefly examines two related aspects of small firms financing that have attracted interest in recent years: venture capital and the activities of 'business angels'. The focus in this chapter is on UK experience, but many of the underlying issues are relevant for other advanced economies.

A term that crops up in this chapter (and indeed, crucially, in the next) is market failure. Such failure may be defined as a situation where the operation of market forces does not bring about a socially optimal outcome.

Small firms finance: some characteristics

In 2003, total lending (term lending and overdrafts) to UK small businesses – defined for these purposes as independent firms with a turnover of less than £1 million – amounted to £38.9 billion (Bank of England 2004: 11). To provide some idea of relative magnitude, this figure may be compared with the total lending to all non-financial corporations in the United Kingdom at June 2004 of £282 billion.[1]

Some financial ratios

Table 8.1 compares some key financial ratios for SMEs with those for the largest firms in Great Britain. It is based on the average for 1989 and 1990 and covers only companies in the non-financial sector. 'Large' companies are those in the top 2000 in terms of capital employed, while 'small' companies are a 1 in 300

Table 8.1 Some financial ratios: small versus large companies, manufacturing and non-manufacturing (average of 1989 and 1990)

Financial ratio	Industrial sector			
	Manufacturing		Non-manufacturing (excl oil)	
	Small	Large	Small	Large
Fixed assets:				
total assets[a]	0.34	0.50	0.31	0.63
Trade debt:				
total assets[b]	0.44	0.28	0.35	0.27
Current liabilities:				
total liabilities	0.55	0.35	0.62	0.30
Trade creditors:				
current liabilities[c]	0.39	0.26	0.34	0.31
Shareholders interests:				
total liabilities	0.36	0.39	0.24	0.47
Short-term loans:				
total loans[d]	0.87	0.64	0.82	0.56

Source: Derived from data in Central Statistical Office (1992: Tables 8 and 9)

Notes: [a] Total net fixed assets as a proportion of total net fixed assets *and* total current assets.
[b] Trade debtors as a proportion of total current assets.
[c] Trade creditors falling due within a year as a proportion of total current liabilities.
[d] Total creditors and accruals falling due within a year as a proportion of total creditors and accruals falling due within a year *and* total creditors and accruals falling due after more than a year.

sample of the rest. Unfortunately the information needed to translate what this means into corresponding employment or sales size bands is not available.

The figures highlight some important small–large firm differences in the structure of corporate financing in the period covered (see also Cosh and Hughes 1994: 34–7). First, small firms tended to have a relatively low fixed assets: total assets ratio, a reflection in part of their generally lower capital intensity. Second, they were likely to have a greater proportion of their assets tied up in trade debt, a characteristic that made them more vulnerable to the financial fortunes of their customers. Third, current liabilities (e.g. bank overdrafts, trade creditors) were relatively much more important as a component of total liabilities. Fourth, trade creditors tended to be of greater significance. Fifth, smaller companies relied less heavily on shareholders to finance their business (especially in non-manufacturing). Finally, smaller companies made relatively more use of short-term loans to support their activities. The overall picture from these data is that small firms tend to be relatively more dependent on short-term financing. The ratios in Table 8.1 provide a ranking of small and large companies that is consistent across the manufacturing and non-manufacturing sectors. (Not surprisingly however, there are variations across the sectors in the absolute value of the ratios and in the differences between small and large companies.)

These figures are not without their limitations. For example, the small–large size divide is arbitrary. Furthermore, the exclusive focus on companies inevitably ignores the vast number of small businesses, particularly at the lower end of the size spectrum, that are unincorporated. In 2004, for example, only about 23 per cent of UK businesses with fewer than fifty employees were incorporated (Small Business Service 2005: Table 2). The figure for businesses run solely by their owners, i.e. the businesses that have no employees, was only 8 per cent.

The data are also now rather old and the source that was used to construct them, sadly, is no longer available.[2] It should be remembered too that the table provides only a snapshot and does not pick up *trends* in financing. As indicated below, small firm financing may have become easier in recent years and this in turn is likely to have affected the structure of firms' balance sheets. It should also be recognised that the years covered by Table 8.1 represented a specific phase – the onset of recession – in the economic cycle. However, it is very unlikely that these factors mean that the broad underlying picture presented in the table is now no longer valid.

External funding

As indicated below, much policy attention has been paid to the demand for and supply of *external* funding for small firms. What is known about such funding? The first point to make is that very substantial numbers of SMEs do not borrow money (e.g. Aston Business School 1991: para 8.31; Reid 1993: 73; Johnson and Conway 1996). Some of the most comprehensive evidence on SME funding comes from Cosh and Hughes (2000b: 46) who found that for the period 1997–9, only about 39 per cent of their SME sample looked for external funding. This percentage does however change significantly from period to period – it was 65 per cent in 1987–90 (see the evidence quoted in Lund and Wright 1999) – suggesting that general economic conditions have an important influence on funding patterns. Cosh and Hughes (2000b: 46) also found that this percentage was higher for larger SMEs, those who are innovating and those who are growing.

The available data on the *sources* of external funding that is obtained suggest a key role for the banks. Cosh and Hughes (2000b: 52) found that overall, 61 per cent of external funds (among SMEs that obtained some external finance) came from this source in 1997–9, although again, as Cosh and Hughes show, this percentage varies over time. The next biggest source of funds came from HP/Leasing (at 23 per cent). There were variations in external funding patterns *within* the SME sector. For example, micro businesses relied relatively more heavily on bank borrowing and relatively less on HP/Leasing (and indeed venture capital) than small or medium-sized businesses. Fast growing SMEs obtained a relatively higher proportion of their funds from the banks than did their counterparts who were stable or declining in size or growing only modestly. Innovators and manufacturers tended to get relatively less of their funds from the banks. These findings emphasise the fact that the characteristics of small businesses are likely to exercise an important influence on the funding they receive.

One of the challenges posed by the kinds of data given in Table 8.1 is how they should be interpreted. In a sense, the data are purely descriptive; they provide no clue as to how they arise (although guesses may be made). They represent the *combined* outcome of supply and demand influences and it is extremely difficult to disentangle the separate effects of these two factors. On the supply side, key factors are likely to be the objectives, efficiency and competitiveness of the financial sector, most notably the banks. Some consideration is given to these issues later in the chapter. On the demand side, the characteristics of small businesses (see above) and the motivations of their owners will play an important role.

The way in which motivations are likely to affect the financial structure of businesses may be illustrated in terms of the widespread desire for independence among small business owners: see for example the evidence in Cosh and Hughes (1994: 26–7). (These authors also show that *loss* of independence or control was by far and away the most important *disadvantage* attributed by owners to take-over.)

Those owners with a strong desire for independence will tend to find debt finance relatively more attractive than equity finance, since the former does not lead to any dilution of ownership control – except in the event of total failure – whereas the latter does. It should also be noted that the desire for independence may affect the particular legal form adopted by the business which in turn will have implications for financing. A business that remains unincorporated for example, has to disclose less information. This may be attractive to independently minded small business owners who want to minimise external 'interference', even though their personal liability remains unlimited. An unincorporated status means however that businesses cannot raise funds from shareholders. The lower disclosure requirements are likely too to make them less attractive to external funders.

Another relevant aspect of motivation likely to affect financing characteristics relates to the orientation of small business owners towards growth. Some of the evidence on such motivation was reviewed in Chapter 6. Firms wanting to grow in a sustained way are more likely to go for longer-term finance, rather than shorter-term arrangements.

The analysis of the influences that give rise to the sort of picture presented in Table 8.1 is made more difficult by the fact that supply and demand conditions change over time. For example, advances in management techniques, notably credit scoring, may have *enhanced* the availability of funds in recent years (see HM Treasury 2004a: 12 fn) by reducing vetting costs and any personal bias introduced into the decisions made by individual bank managers. (For a fascinating study of the potential for variation in decisions on loans across bank managers, see Deakins and Hussain 1993.)

Investigations into small firm funding in the United Kingdom: the historical record

Some 'landmark' reports

There is a long history of discussion of 'gaps' in the provision of small firm finance and given the policy importance of such phenomena, it may be helpful briefly to review the historical development of this discussion in the United Kingdom, as this development serves to illustrate some of the key issues. The Macmillan Committee Report on Finance and Industry (Macmillan Committee 1931: para 404) identified what came to be known as the 'Macmillan gap' for long-term finance for SMEs for amounts of up to around £200,000 (in 2006 prices, equivalent to over £9 million – a considerable sum, except for the largest SME). For sums of this nature, the cost of a public issue was too large relative to the amount of capital raised. Following the Macmillan Report, a number of new institutions were set up in the 1930s, although their contribution to small firm finance was relatively small (Bolton Committee 1971: para 12.8).

After the Second World War however a much more significant development occurred with the creation, in 1946, of the Industrial and Commercial Finance Corporation (ICFC) by the London clearing banks, the Scottish Banks and the Bank of England. A key function of the ICFC was 'to provide credit . . . where the existing facilities provided by banking institutions and the Stock Exchanges are not readily or easily available' (Radcliffe Committee 1958: para 943). This was interpreted then as meaning funding between £5000 and £200,000 (approximately £80,000 to £3.1 million in 2006 prices).

When the Radcliffe Committee on the Working of the Monetary System reported on its deliberations over small firms at the end of the 1950s (Radcliffe Committee 1958: 932–52), it made a number of recommendations to enhance further the finance available to these firms,[3] recommendations that were largely implemented.

Because of these developments, the Bolton Committee of Inquiry on Small Firms felt able to conclude in 1971 that although the new issue market still remained effectively closed for small sums, there had been a general improvement in the availability of longer term finance for small firms (Bolton Committee 1971: para 12.7f). The Committee also took the general view that although relative to larger firms, the small firm faced a number of disadvantages in raising finance, these disadvantages mostly 'reflect[ed] the higher costs of lending in small amounts or the higher risk of lending to small borrowers; they do not result from imperfections in the supply of finance' (para 12.98). As a result, the Committee did not recommend the creation of any new institutions or the provision of subsidised finance for small firms.

At the end of the 1970s, the Wilson Committee on the Functioning of Financial Institutions (Wilson Committee 1979) came to a somewhat different conclusion and recommended the introduction, on an experimental basis, of a Small Business (now Firms) Loan Guarantee Scheme (SFLGS) which would provide government guarantees for bank lending to small firms. However the case for the SFLGS was put in rather weak terms: the Committee

> was *sufficiently uncertain* about the effectiveness of competition between the clearing banks for small firm business to believe there to be *a reasonable chance* that a publicly underwritten scheme would generate a desirable increase in the volume of lending to viable small businesses.
>
> (Wilson Committee 1979: para 29; italics added)

The SFLGS was set up in 1981 and has been in operation ever since. In 2006, it was offering a 75 per cent guarantee to the lender for loans up to £250,000.

A focus on particular types of small firm

The issue has been revisited regularly since the Wilson Report, and a number of new measures have been introduced in addition to the SFLGS. The focus of the debate has moved away somewhat from a *general* treatment of 'gaps' to financing issues associated with particular types of small business. Two such types that have received attention in recent years are technology-based small firms (TBSFs) and start-up and 'early stage' businesses.

The first of these topics, TBSFs, was the subject of a Bank of England (1996) report and then of a report of a working group chaired by Sir Peter Williams, of Oxford Instruments Group plc in 1998 (see the reference in Bank of England 2001: 57). The Bank of England published its own second report on TBSFs three years later (Bank of England 2001). It is instructive to note the conclusions of the literature review in this second report:

> this review has emphasised that the information asymmetries, moral hazard and adverse selection that feature in aspects of SME financing potentially apply with particular force to the provision of start-up and early-stage finance to TBSFs. This reflects the key characteristics of high-tech companies, notably that their value derives mainly from growth options, they lack tangible assets in the early stages of their life cycles which may be used as collateral, and their products are usually subject to high obsolescence rates. These factors are compounded by the greater difficulty finance providers face in assessing the technology, and the greater uncertainties over both the cost of R&D and the prospective demand for the new product. But the empirical evidence on whether all this implies a major gap in the provision of funds to TBSFs, and if so whether this constitutes a market failure, remains inconclusive. Furthermore, even those studies suggesting that lack of access to finance is a greater problem for TBSFs than SMEs generally do not indicate that many TBSFs are particularly concerned over the recent and current financing environment in the UK.
>
> (Bank of England 2001: 98)

This quotation highlights three potential problems that may be particularly relevant for TBSFs, but which may also be present to a greater or lesser degree in SME financing generally. The first, asymmetric information, arises where the small firm applicant and its potential lender may have different information sets about the business. It may be very difficult for the lender to secure the relevant information if the small business owner does not disclose it or to assess the accuracy of the information that is disclosed. Second, moral hazard may occur where the lending of money serves to *reduce* the incentive for owners to perform to the best of their ability, because they know that it is not their finance that they are managing. Third, adverse selection may arise when it is only those businesses with the higher risk that remain in the market for finance as the cost of that finance rises. The lower risk businesses drop out of the market, because the returns appropriate to their lower risk are unable to cover the higher costs. The implications of adverse selection in relation to credit rationing are considered later in the chapter.

The quotation above also emphasises, in a very clear way, the crucially important distinction between the existence of financial problems and challenges reported by small firms and the presence of financial 'gaps'. The first does not necessarily imply the latter. The quotation rightly implies that even where some form of 'gap' is identified, it does not always follow that the market is failing. These issues are explored further in Chapter 9.

The second topic on which discussion on small firms financing has been focused is on the particular financial challenges that start-ups and early stage businesses face: see for example the Graham Review of the SFLGS (HM Treasury 2004a, 2004b). New businesses by definition lack a track record and it may therefore be difficult to raise funds where a cash injection cannot be provided by the owner or security offered. A viable young business may also find it difficult to raise funds for further development even though it has been trading, because it may still lack appropriate resources or security (see HM Treasury 2004b: 17f).

The presence of particular difficulties for new and young firms receives some confirmation from data on the SFLGS which shows that a disproportionate amount of the loans under this scheme goes to start-ups and from the fact that access to finance is the barrier most frequently cited by those setting up in business (see the evidence cited in HM Treasury 2004a: 9). Again, however care must be taken in labelling such a barrier as market failure.

Financial 'gaps': some supply and demand analysis

It is difficult from the above history of special investigations into the financing of small firms in the United Kingdom, to identify a clear concept of a financial 'gap'. In the following discussion, some basic supply and demand analysis is used to clarify the concept and to suggest possible ways in which in principle it might be measured. There are numerous angles from which the issue might be approached. Just five of many possible interpretations of 'gaps' are examined.

In each one, the question of whether or not market failure exists is also briefly addressed.

Before this is done however, an explanatory note on the diagrams that follow is necessary. The vertical axis measures the cost of the loan, r. The horizontal axis measures the amount of funding per period, denoted by F. For the moment, a competitive market is assumed, i.e. no single buyer or seller, or group of buyers or sellers, is able to exercise any influence over the market; they have to take the market price as a given.

On the demand side, a distinction is made between private demand, D_{pri}, and public (or social) demand D_{pub}. The former represents the aggregate demand schedule of small businesses themselves. The latter is the demand schedule for small firm funding of society as a whole. The precise measurement of social demand is a complex matter, but the following analysis is not dependent on resolving this (very real) issue. Where private and social demand are identical (see Figures 8.1 to 8.3), the implication is that there are no benefits for society from small firm funding over and above those accruing to the businesses themselves. In the jargon of economics there are no 'positive externalities' of small firm funding. Where they diverge, the private market outcome would result in a market equilibrium that is sub-optimal from society's viewpoint. (It is assumed – for the sake of simplicity – that in all the scenarios illustrated, private supply equals public (or social) supply. Subscripts for the supply schedule are not therefore included.)

The market clears at the equilibrium price, r_e.[4]

Some interpretations of financial 'gaps' may now be outlined.

A 'gap' arising from an unwillingness of small firms to pay the market price

Small businesses may report – for example, in surveys – that they are unable to obtain the funds they want. For some of them, however, this difficulty may simply be a reflection of their unwillingness to pay the going market rate. This possibility may be illustrated with the help of Figure 8.1. Those firms located somewhere on the demand schedule below the equilibrium price, r_e, would like to obtain funds, but only at a price lower than r_e. Such firms may nevertheless report 'difficulties' or 'problems' over raising funds. For the measurement of such a 'gap' to be make any sense, a price such as r_1 needs to be specified. Two options for measuring this 'gap' at price r_1 are $F_2 - F_e$ or $F_2 - F_1$.

The problem with this notion of a 'gap' is that it does not of itself have much economic significance, certainly if no other case is made for supplying subsidised funding to small firms. After all, most businesses (and indeed individuals) would prefer to obtain finance at below the market price, preferably at a zero price! Yet it is sometimes difficult to avoid the impression that at least some of the arguments for providing special financial assistance to small firms boil down to unhappiness at the market rate on offer. In this scenario, the market can hardly be said to be failing.

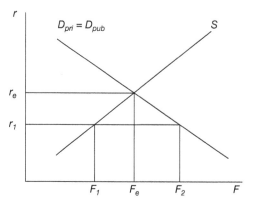

Figure 8.1 A 'gap' arising from an unwillingness of small firms to pay the market price

A 'gap' arising from higher costs of supplying finance to small businesses, compared with large firms

By the nature of things, the provision of funds to small firms may be relatively more costly than that to large firms, a point made by the Bolton Committee (1971) in its deliberations (see p. 104). The higher costs may reflect a number of factors. First, there are fixed costs of approving funds. The costs of vetting applications do not increase proportionately with the amount of funds involved. On top of these cost disadvantages, there are specific small firm costs: smaller firms may be inherently more risky; and there may be greater asymmetry of information between the firm and the lender than with large firms. For example, smaller firms tend to be less subject to external appraisal by independent agencies than larger ones.

Second, there are fixed costs of assessing and monitoring: the cost for example of evaluating the financial information contained in the annual report and accounts of an applicant firm with £10 million turnover is unlikely to be ten times the costs of dealing with the report and accounts of a firm of £1 million turnover. There may be particular problems with TBSFs especially if they are new, that raise assessment and monitoring costs. New technologies and their potential markets may be more expensive to assess, especially in the early phase; and risks may be higher. These problems may be exacerbated by the possibility that an applicant may be reluctant to disclose the details of a technology to a potential funder for fear that the information may 'leak' to a competitor.

Where the costs of supplying small firms with finance are higher than those of supplying large firms, the resultant 'gap' may be illustrated with the help of Figure 8.2. The actual supply schedule for small firm funding is given by S, as in Figure 8.1. S^* is the supply schedule for such funding that would exist if the costs of supplying small firms were the same as those incurred from supplying large firms. Thus at any given price, more would be supplied to small firms with S^* than with S. Two possible measures of the 'gap' are $F_2 - F_e$ or $F_2 - F_1$.

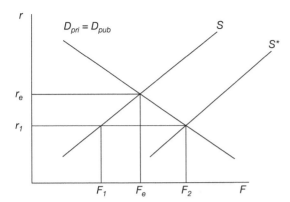

Figure 8.2 A 'gap' arising from higher costs of supplying finance to small businesses, compared with large firms

The higher costs implied by S are however a fact of economic life. They do not, of themselves, suggest that the market is failing, although policymakers may take the view, based on other factors, that F_e is sub-optimal from a social point of view.

A 'gap' arising from credit rationing

So far it has been assumed that the demand and supply schedules have the conventional slopes. However this may not always be the case. Consider Figure 8.3.

At r_e, the quantities of F demanded and supplied are equal. However, unusually, financial institutions are willing to supply more at a *lower r*. Indeed the supply of F would in fact be maximised at r^*. The rate of interest charged is less than the market-clearing rate because it provides a higher return to the lender. Credit rationing results: borrowers willing to pay r^* cannot get the funds.

What might lead to such a scenario? A full technical explanation of why the situation illustrated in Figure 8.3 might arise cannot be provided here, although the underlying reasoning may be briefly outlined. (The seminal article here is Stiglitz and Weiss 1981; Hillier and Ibrahimo 1993 also have an excellent treatment of the topic.)

A key assumption behind Figure 8.3 is that there is asymmetry in the information held by the lender and the borrower when it comes to the projects for which the latter is seeking financial help. The lenders are assumed not to know the probability of success of a project or indeed, the financial returns to the borrowing firm that would arise if the project were to be successful, whereas it is assumed that information is available to the would-be borrower. So the lender is ignorant of the risk involved. As a result, it is unable to distinguish between high risk and low risk projects. It charges the same interest

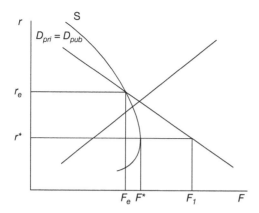

Figure 8.3 A 'gap' arising from credit rationing

rate for its funds to all comers. It is also assumed that if the project fails the lender loses its money, whereas if the project is successful, it will simply receive the interest on the loan. Hence the borrower either pays nothing if the project fails or receives any excess over and above the interest if it succeeds.

Now as the interest rate rises there will be two conflicting forces at work. On the one hand, higher interest rates will increase the return to the lender because of the higher repayments. So the lender will be willing to lend more. On the other hand, the higher interest rate will act as a disincentive for firms with low risk, low returns, to seek finance. They will tend to drop out of the market whereas the more risky projects, which if successful could generate high enough returns to pay the interest rate charged by the lender, will remain in. The lender will find its portfolio increasingly populated with riskier projects. As the interest rate rises, there will come a point where the losses from the riskier projects outweigh the higher returns from the higher rate. Thus as the interest rate rises, the lender will become less willing to provide funding. The turning point occurs at interest rate r^* in Figure 8.3 and credit rationing results. Lenders are unwilling to raise their rates, even though demands exceeds supply, because they would reduce their profits. It is important to note however that whether or not rationing occurs will depend on the shape of the supply curve. It is not difficult to envisage a scenario where r^* lies above r_e.

There are a number of features of this model that should be noted in the context of small firms. First, it is of course relevant only where businesses are seeking to borrow money. As already indicated, many small business owners may not wish to do so.

Second, the lender is seen as being at arm's length from the borrower: it is not involved in its business, and thus does not influence outcomes. Furthermore, the type of contract that is implied is one where the lender cannot alter things if the project is beginning to look like a failure.

Third, no collateral is involved. Collateral may well alter the lender–borrower relationship in a number of ways. Most obviously, it reduces or eliminates any potential losses that the lender would incur from a failed project. Collateral may also make the would-be borrower more committed to the project, as more is at stake if the project is unsuccessful. In addition, it may convey an important signal to the lender about the project, as borrowers are unlikely to put up collateral if they think that the risks of failure are high. In other words, the provision of collateral may be seen as a mechanism for identifying borrowers with good projects.

Fourth, at the heart of the credit rationing model is the presence of asymmetries in information. How important are such asymmetries? Banks do of course have a range of measures available to them to increase the information that they have, yet it is highly unlikely that they will be as well informed on a project being undertaken by a well-established company as the company itself will be. However when it comes to *small* businesses it is not at all clear that the bank will be necessarily *less* well informed. It is of course true that less public information is available on smaller businesses, because of the type of legal form they adopt, but the businesses are often less complex. It may also be the case that where small businesses are young, owners are relatively ignorant about both their own business abilities and the market in which they are operating. Following Jovanovic (1982), owners may of course learn through time, as they extend their experience of market operations, but at the beginning, their bank may be *more* knowledgeable about the nature of their business and prospects for success. Eventually of course the small business owner may get to the point where the asymmetry puts the bank in a weaker position along the lines specified in the model.

Where credit rationing of the type identified in Figure 8.3 exists, the resultant 'gap' may be measured as $F_1 - F^*$. The market may be said to be failing in the sense that firms, with viable projects and willing to pay r^* are neverthless denied funding.

A 'gap' arising because the market is not fully competitive

In the cases so far examined, a competitive market has been assumed. However another kind of 'gap' may arise where financial institutions have market power and are thus able to raise prices beyond their competitive level.

There is some evidence that at least in England and Wales, competition in the supply of funds to SMEs at least in recent years has not been as strong it might have been: Competition Commission (2002). The Commission found that price competition among the clearing banks in the supply of banking services to SMEs was restricted and distorted and that this led to excessive prices and profits. They also found significant barriers to entry and growth for liquidity management services and general purpose business loans. It proposed some remedies (e.g. the encouragement of easier switching by customers) and the banks made a number of undertakings designed to remedy excessive profits and prices and to encourage price competition.[5] It is interesting to note however that notwithstanding its finding of excessive profits and prices, the Competition

Commission reported that 'the cost and availability of lending [to SMEs] are in general not a problem' (Competition Commission 2002: para 1.6).

Any 'gap' arising from market power might best be defined as the difference between the 'competitive' F and the 'market power' F (not illustrated here). The market fails in the sense that the presence of market power means that not all those small firms who are prepared to cover the competitive level of costs of being supplied with finance are in fact supplied.

A 'gap' arising because social demand exceeds private demand

Figure 8.4 captures the situation where at each price, private demand exceeds social demand. In other words, at any given r, society as a whole has a greater demand for funds than does the small firms sector.

There may be a number of reasons why the social demand for funds might exceed the private demand. The earlier discussion on the particular challenges faced by start-ups and early stage businesses and by TBSFs gives some clues. For example, a young small firm might well prove to be viable and to act as an important source of competition and economic growth if it could get over the initial birth and neo-natal phase, when it is at its most vulnerable to shocks and reaction by existing companies and when it is restricted, for the reasons given earlier, in its ability to raise funds. Thus social demand for funds, based on an assessment of the future contribution of the firm to competitiveness and economic growth, may thus be higher than that of the firm itself. Similar arguments may apply with even greater force to TBSFs. A fuller treatment of externalities is provided in Chapter 9; the primary concern here is with how a financial gap might arise and be measured.

In Figure 8.4, the equilibrium price in the market is, as before, r_e. In this scenario, a gap resulting from demand side externalities is generated although, again, there are ambiguities about how the gap should be measured. Two

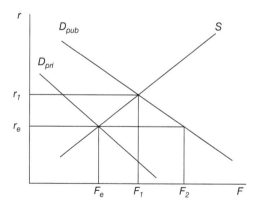

Figure 8.4 A 'gap' arising from a divergence between public and social demand

alternatives are $F_2 - F_e$ or $F_1 - F_e$. The market fails to produce the socially optimal amount of small firm funding.

Review

A number of possible interpretations of financial 'gaps' have been suggested, only some of which may be regarded as potentially giving rise to market failure. Overall and not withstanding the Competition Commission's strictures, however, it would be difficult to argue, especially given the presence of competition authorities, that there is any evidence of *systemic* failure in the market for funds to SMEs in the United Kingdom. However in two specific markets – the funding of TBSFs and of new or young businesses – there are some good arguments to suggest that the competitive 'private' outcome would be suboptimal. It should be stressed again however that the presence of such failure is not *itself* sufficient grounds for arguing that intervention should follow, a point taken up in Chapter 9.

Venture capital

Much has been made of the growth of venture capital companies as a source of funding for SMEs, yet the main focus of these companies is fairly specific: the provision of medium to long-term equity investment in unquoted companies that are perceived as having high growth potential. The returns to this funding are typically realised by sale or public flotation. Venture capital funding focuses on the seed to expansion stages of business investment whereas other sources of private equity include, for example, buy-outs and buy-ins. For further discussion of terms see British Venture Capital Association (BVCA) (2004).

The 165 or so members of the BVCA represent the vast majority of private equity and venture capital funders in the United Kingdom. In 2003, members invested about £6.4 billion in just under 1500 businesses, at home and abroad (BVCA 2004). It is worth noting however that start-up and 'other' early stage investment amounted to less than 5 per cent of the total whereas buy-outs and buy-ins accounted for over 46 per cent.

Average funding provided for businesses at the start-up stage was estimated at £0.4 million, considerably larger than that provided to start-ups funded by business angels (see next section). The new businesses being assisted by BVCA members are clearly of a significant scale when compared with the general run of formations. It is also the case that while venture capital may be of critical importance to the firms who receive it, it is irrelevant or inappropriate for the vast majority of SMEs.

Business angels

In recent years the 'informal' capital market has received increasing attention. Key players in that market are business angels, defined by Mason and Harrison

(2002a: 272) as 'high net worth individuals (mostly self-made) who invest their own money in unlisted businesses'. These authors have also provided a wealth of detail on the activities of such investors. They *conservatively* estimate (Mason and Harrison 2000) that in 1998–9 there were 20,000 business angels in the United Kingdom, investing £0.5 billion per annum in 3000 businesses.[6] The amounts involved are clearly small relative to the scale of investment by venture capitalists. Not surprisingly, business angels tend to be wealthy: 71 per cent of those surveyed by Mason and Harrison (2002a) had a net worth, excluding their principal residence, of over £0.5 million and 62 per cent were millionaires. Significantly, they tended to be those who had obtained their wealth through their own efforts, typically in business. Their investment motives are mixed, but financial returns represent the strongest motivation followed by the non-financial returns obtained from being directly involved in a business venture.

Compared with venture capital funds, business angels tend to invest relatively small amounts – typically, under £100,000 in the United Kingdom (under $200,000 in the United States): see Mason and Harrison (2000). As these authors also point out, business angels tend to focus rather more on the start-up and early development phases of business activity and to get actively involved in the businesses they support. The returns to these investments are mixed. The evidence suggests that while a small minority of projects yield very handsome returns, a substantial proportion – perhaps nearly half – only break even or make losses (Mason and Harrison 2002b).

Mason and Harrison (2002a) present evidence that business angels are willing to invest significantly more than they currently do in business activity. They suggest that at the time they undertook their survey, members of the (then) National Business Angels Network (now the British Business Angels Association), an organisation that covers many key players, might have another £70 million to invest. Survey respondents also indicated that they would be willing to change the structure of their assets portfolio to reflect this additional investment. At the same time, however, Mason and Harrison (2002a) point out that because of the mismatch between the investment criteria of business angels and the characteristics of the potential borrowers who are seeking funds; the poor quality of investment proposals, as perceived by the angels; and the difficulty of negotiating acceptable terms and conditions, this willingness to lend does not translate into actual loans.

It is a little difficult to know how to interpret the finding that business angels would be prepared to lend more if there were more applicants who met their criteria. It is not necessarily evidence of market failure. It simply indicates that 'good' proposals, *as defined by business angels*, would receive funding, a result that has something of the tautological about it. In terms of Figure 8.1, those business angels willing to lend more than they actually do lend, may be located on that section of the supply schedule that is above the equilibrium price, r_e.

Concluding comment

Small firms have a number of distinctive financial characteristics, which reflect numerous influences including the inherent cost disadvantages that they may face in raising funds and the kinds of objectives that motivate their owners. At the same time, their very smallness may offer access to funds from business angels that are unavailable to their larger counterparts.

There has been much discussion of the difficulties faced by small firms in raising external finance and of the presence of financial 'gaps'. This chapter has shown however that the concept of a financial 'gap' is capable of a range of interpretations. It has also argued that there is little firm evidence that the financial market is failing SMEs in any significant sense. If there are potential problem areas, it is with TBSFs and early stage businesses.

9 Issues in policy

Introduction

Since the early 1980s there has been a very substantial increase in measures designed to support small firms. Today, such support is expressed in a wide-ranging, and some would say, bewildering, raft of initiatives and institutions. For example, in the United Kingdom in June 2006, the on-line Grant and Support Directory of Business Link, the UK government funded business support agency, listed 2746 potential sources of help – including private sector initiatives. The Directory permits some fine tuning for particular types of need, location and sector. An illustration of the greater precision that is possible may be helpful: someone from Durham City (in the North of England) wanting help in June 2006 in setting up in 'Manufacturing and Engineering' could potentially make use of nine grant schemes, seven awards, twenty-six loan types and sixteen sources of advice from consultants.[1] The type of help available included financial assistance and free or subsidised services, ranging from advice to practical involvement with projects. Many of these measures were small scale, and not all businesses were eligible for all types of support, but the figures nevertheless give some idea of the overall extent and complexity of small business support activity. Alongside these forms of support are many hard copy and/or online sources of free advice.

Numerous agencies have been used or created to deliver policy initiatives and/or to formulate policy. In UK central government alone, one study identified fifteen Departments with 265 programmes aimed at small business (quoted in National Audit Office 2006: 4). In addition, local government, Regional Development Agencies (RDAs), Enterprise Agencies, Learning and Skills Councils, quasi commercial bodies set up specifically to assist small business in areas affected by major redundancies or deprivation, trade bodies, such as Chambers of Commerce, have all been involved. In addition, government has used commercial organisations to deliver some of its support. In the United Kingdom, the best example of this kind of policy conduit is the Small Firms Loan Guarantee Scheme (see pp. 104–5).

The resources devoted to small firm support are substantial. In the United Kingdom in 2003–4, for example, the total costs of services to small firms were estimated by a government review as nearly £2.5 billion (National Audit Office 2006: 1). These estimates are gross figures in the sense that they do not take account of the fact that without support, many small businesses might not survive and hence the tax take would be lower. If payments to farmers under the Common Agricultural Policy and tax relief are included, the figure rises dramatically: nearly £8 billion in 2001–2 (HM Treasury and Small Business Service 2002a).

The United Kingdom is far from being alone in the development of small firm policies, as can be seen from an international OECD (2005) survey which examined these policies in twenty-nine advanced countries, including the United States, and at EU level. The survey demonstrated a widespread policy commitment to encouraging small firm development, and an extensive range of policy interventions, both within and across countries.

The precise portfolio of initiatives and agencies does of course change over time as political priorities, personnel and the state of knowledge change. It is not intended therefore to catalogue the details of particular current measures, which might have only a short shelf life anyway. Instead, the underlying issues associated with small business support will be examined. In the next section, the case for policy intervention is considered. The third section looks at policy delivery mechanisms. The fourth section raises issues relating to the evaluation of policy.

The case for policy intervention

Support for small firms may be offered for political reasons. For example, the owners of such firms may be seen by politicians as an important constituency to woo for electoral support. The small firm lobby may also be sufficiently strong for politicians to perceive it as one that they can ignore only at their peril. More fundamentally, the encouragement of the individualism inherent in small business may be seen as an important mechanism for defending democratic values and institutions and as a counter balance to the pressures exerted by large corporations. Furthermore, where small firms are perceived as providing important economic benefits, particularly in terms of jobs, governments may find it in their own political interests to encourage such activity.

It is important to bear these factors in mind as they provide a useful counter to the notion that purely economic arguments dominate the policy agenda. Further analysis of these political influences however mostly lies outside the scope of this chapter, although some reference is made later to the way in which the objectives of politicians and policymakers can lead to 'government failure'. Here the focus is on the economic arguments for the public support of small firms.

Market failure arguments

These arguments hinge on the presence of some form of market failure (see p. 100). Chapter 8 looked at possibilities of market failure in the specific context of financial markets; here the concern is with the wider context: whether market forces are likely to lead to a socially optimal outcome as far as formation activity, the survival of small businesses and their growth are concerned. Market failure may occur for a number of reasons.

First, there may be 'external' benefits (or costs) that the new or small firm generates but which do not accrue in full to its owner. Since a business owner will tend to make decisions based only on that portion of the benefits and costs that get reflected in his or her accounts, the outcomes in situations where 'externalities' exist are likely to be socially sub-optimal in the sense that decisions are not made on the basis of *all* benefits (and costs).

Positive externalities may derive from a number of sources. For example, a new or small firm may generate a technological development from which other firms may benefit by 'free-riding', i.e. using the development without paying for it. Again, there may be agglomeration benefits from the presence of a small firm in a particular location. Where small firms are clustered together in spatial terms, suppliers servicing these firms may be more likely to locate near to them and the local labour force may be more attuned to their needs. A good deal of research has also demonstrated the importance of geographical clustering when it comes to innovative activity in small firms (OECD 2005: 130f). These agglomeration benefits mean that the impact of an individual small firm is in fact greater than it would make if it were 'free standing'. (Some care must however be exercised in any evaluation of agglomeration benefits, since it would be expected that in a competitive market, rents would rise to reflect the greater benefits that would be obtained.)

Similar effects may be felt on the demand side. The advent of a new retailer in a shopping centre for example, may generate additional sales in the centre over and above its own, simply because consumers are more willing to visit the shopping centre because of the greater choice it offers as a result of a new arrival.

A further externality may arise through the social benefits associated with the generation of employment. Such activity may itself cause those who move from unemployed to employed status as a result to have a higher sense of self-worth and lower anxiety levels. There is survey evidence to suggest for example that reported happiness levels rise significantly when people cease to be unemployed (see Layard 2005: 64). Benefits of a similar kind may arise if a self-employed person is able to stay in business rather than be forced out. Business failure can be a source of significant grieving (Shepherd 2003), with all the consequences that this may imply for others. These sorts of benefits are notoriously difficult to measure but they have important positive knock-on effects on others.

In addition, a positive externality may be generated where a small firm has a 'role model' effect on other would-be founders. A successful small firm may serve to demonstrate that the formation of a business is a practical possibility and that the returns can be good. This may be one explanation behind Mueller's (2005) finding – for Germany – that higher levels of new and small firm activity in a region may encourage people who are thinking about becoming self-employed actually to become so. It may also underpin the evidence that the spin-off rate of new firm founders tends to be higher in smaller firms and plants (see p. 61). This role model externality may be of particular significance in communities where, for historical reasons, there is a cultural bias against self-employment. There may, however, also be negative impacts from this demonstration effect. For example, where a business is set up and then fails, others may be less inclined to embark on small-scale activity. Again, the demonstration effect may lead to an oversupply of small businesses to a particular market. This may occur where those who follow do not realise that many others are making decisions similar to those that they themselves are making.

Second, there may be 'infant firm' arguments. Here the argument is that a fledgling small firm may need some form of support in its early stages of life, so that it can establish its own viability and become self-sustaining. It may for example be unable to operate initially at a level that takes advantage of all the economies of scale available. If the firm were to develop too rapidly from birth in order to reach optimum size, it might run into major management difficulties. Yet once established, the firm may become a powerful competitive force in its own right. Another problem may arise over the new or young firm's inability to offer collateral when applying for external funding: such a business may have few assets.

Third, there may be information problems. These may take various forms. Potential owners may not themselves be aware of their own abilities and the returns that might be made from small-scale business. Attention has already been drawn (p. 35) to the learning effects of actual business experience. By definition, would-be founders do not have access to this information source in respect of the particular business they are planning, although 'serial entrepreneurs' will have learnt something about themselves and business from their previous activities: see Stam et al. (2005). In the absence of previous experience, potential founders may have only a poor perception of the business opportunities available to them, or a very distorted view of these opportunities. They may not be aware of their *own* abilities and limitations as business owners and managers. Provision of information and training may help here although such services are unlikely to be a perfect substitute for actual experience. It is of course important to recognise that incomplete information is a characteristic of virtually all business situations. A central question for policymakers in this kind of situation then becomes how much *additional* information should be supplied by the public purse.

Information deficiencies are not confined to small business owners. Financial institutions may not be as aware as they might be of the nature of small business operations and the financial challenges that they pose. Furthermore, in the case of new firms, the information embedded in the willingness to provide collateral may simply not be available. Again however it is important to remember in any discussion of information, that *perfect* information would be a very costly, if not an impossible goal. Some forms of credit rationing (see pp. 109–11) may be an inevitable consequence. Furthermore, it is reasonable to suppose that the more competitive financial markets are, the more financial institutions will be forced towards optimal information provision. The policy issue here is the competitiveness of the financial sector.

The costs of policy intervention

Some market failure arguments have been outlined above. Even if some or all of these arguments have empirical validity, *it does not necessarily follow that policy intervention is justified*. Such justification is possible only when these benefits are judged to *exceed the costs of the intervention*. Thus the presence of benefits is not by itself enough to justify an intervention, since the costs of obtaining these – by putting right the market failure – may exceed the costs of the failure itself. Part of the costs of policy may be those arising from 'government failure'. This type of failure may occur, where the involvement of public bodies leads to a waste of resources, through, for example, duplication across departments and the development of complex administrative procedures and overlapping sets of objectives (see National Audit Office 2006 for consideration of some of the complexities of small firms policy delivery in the United Kingdom).

Government failure may also occur if funding is used to support businesses that do not require it and whose behaviour is not affected by the assistance. To the extent that the latter occurs, 'deadweight' is said to characterise the policy intervention. Some work by Ernst and Young (quoted in Bryson et al. 1999) on subsidised consultancy to SMEs through Business Link suggested that nearly half of recipients would have used alternative sources if this service had not been available, suggesting substantial deadweight in the case of this service.

Government failure may arise too where public bodies vie with each other to support small business. The officials running the government departments or agencies concerned may wish to promote the long run growth and survival of their own organisations and this in turn may distort priorities.

How the balance of benefits and costs works out for any particular policy will of course be an empirical matter. A policy may still be worthwhile even when it appears that it is generating unwanted costs. For example, although the Graham Review of the SFLGS (HM Treasury 2004a: 26) showed that the scheme's default rate is around 30–35 per cent – about 60 per cent in 1989–90 – compared with around 4 per cent on secured lending to SMEs, it does not necessarily follow from this fact alone, that the scheme, overall, is not worthwhile. The losses may be more than compensated for by the gains.

Policy delivery mechanisms

The way in which policy is delivered may have an important impact on how effective it is in achieving its goals and on its worthwhileness in social cost benefit terms. This section looks at the options for policy delivery. There are at least five sets of key choices that policymakers face.

What target?

The first is the choice between delivery that targets specific small firm issues and one that seeks to change the general social and economic environment within which such firms operate. This environment would include the regulatory framework (e.g. employment health and safety legislation) and general economic conditions. See Kingston University (2005) for a good review of the costs and benefits of regulating small firms.

A tailored or blanket approach?

A second set of choices arises if it is decided that policy is going to specifically target small firms. In the case of regulation, such an approach would translate into a preferential treatment of small firms, for example by the granting of exemptions or the imposition of less demanding regulatory conditions. The classic case here is exemption from the need to register for VAT in the United Kingdom if sales are under the VAT threshold. There is then a choice to be made between delivery that is based on an assessment of the needs and circumstances of individual small firms and delivery that is applied in a blanket fashion to small firms as a whole. The latter approach is based on firms qualifying for assistance simply on the basis of certain characteristics. A critical question here is, how far can policies be tailor-made to suit particular small businesses?

Superficially, 'targeting' policy measures appears an attractive option, not least because resources only then flow to those who will benefit from them. However such an approach presupposes an ability on the part of policymakers to identify suitable target individuals and firms without at the same time including other firms who would not benefit from policy assistance. The evidence suggests that caution should be exercised in making such an assumption. For example, Robson and Bennett (2000) show that there is no significant relationship between the use of Business Link services and client performance, even though these services were intended to be targeted on firms with growth potential.[2]

There is a further point. Even if governments *could* identify individuals and firms most likely to benefit, the administrative costs of so doing may be prohibitive. In other words it may be more efficient to pursue a blanket policy, even though some policy resources may be 'wasted'.

What type of small firm?

The third 'tier' of choices relates to the *types* of small firms that are targeted. Examples of possible foci might be high tech, new, or manufacturing small firms. Different categories of firms may experience different forms of market failure. The Graham Review of the SFLGS (HM Treasury 2004b: 19) suggested for example that the scheme should be targeted at start-ups and early stage businesses because this was where financial difficulties in raising funds were most concentrated.

What aspect of small firm development?

The fourth set of choices, which again assumes that the small firm is the specific target, relates to the particular aspect of small firm development that is targeted. Figure 9.1 illustrates the five main policy options that in turn may be grouped under three intervention categories. (Employment is used as the measure of development in Figure 9.1; other measures could of course be used.) First, policy may seek to alter the start date, to delay it – for example, to ensure that a potential owner is sufficiently trained before embarking on a business venture – or to bring it forward, so that the gains from a new formation can be realised more quickly. Under this heading attempts to both discourage and encourage people thinking of going into business may be included. Discouraging those whose plans are unlikely to be viable and encouraging those who could develop successful business activities but who may not have thought of doing so (or who have done so, but lack confidence) has obvious benefits.

Second, policy may be targeted on the finish date, usually seeking to extend it, i.e. increasing the likelihood of survival. Finally, policy may be focused on different aspects of the profile between birth and death. Intervention may be designed to affect the early growth phase, size at maturity or the rate of decline.

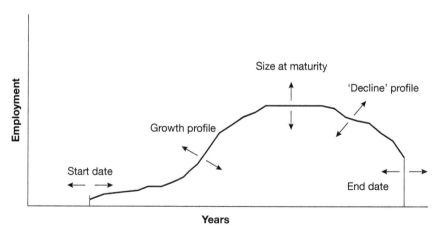

Figure 9.1 Growth profile and policy

It should not be assumed here that *higher* initial growth, a *higher* level of activity in the mature phase, or a *lower* rate of decline should necessarily be the policy objective. Slower initial development for example may enhance the long-term sustainability of the business. A smaller 'mature' size may sometimes be preferable on cost grounds. Again, a quick business death may be more efficient than a long drawn out decline. As these examples suggest – the start and finish dates and the various elements of the profile in between – are likely to be interrelated.

What institutional framework?

The fifth set of choices relates to the institutional framework within which policy is delivered. Who should deliver it? The options are wide ranging. Central government, local government, regional development agencies, other quasi public agencies and private sector contractors or some combination of these are the main possibilities. Each of these channels has its advantages and disadvantages. For example, central government is able to take an overview of the national interest and trends, but it is less likely to be aware of local conditions on the ground. The reverse is likely to be true of local government. Again, the profit motive of private sector contractors may lead to a greater emphasis on achieving efficiency gains in the delivery of policy where such gains have a positive effect on their bottom line. The downside may be that they may have little incentive to look at the broader picture.

The evaluation of policy

Different approaches

Policy evaluation may be conducted at a number of levels. Actual performance may simply be evaluated against the (implied or explicit) objectives of policy measures and any targets that are set. Targets may be expressed in a number of ways, e.g. in the case of financial assistance, it might be the numbers applying for assistance; the numbers given assistance; the amount paid out; the number of projects assisted; the satisfaction generated among clients; or the economic impact, e.g. employment, associated with the assistance (a measure that can be variously interpreted). A further variant on this kind of evaluation is assessments of impact or levels of satisfaction recorded by clients.

It is this kind of evaluation that has been undertaken by Bennett and Robson (1999, 2003), Robson and Bennett (2000) and Bennett et al. (2001). These authors have looked at a wide variety of issues surrounding the provision of government sponsored advice for small firms, particularly through the Business Link initiative. They have for example examined the usage, impact – as perceived by the client – and level of client satisfaction that this initiative has had and at their determinants. They point out that while usage has been high, impact and satisfaction levels have been disappointing, with a high level of variability in these levels. Not surprisingly, their results suggest that a key factor in explaining the performance of Business Link is likely to be the quality of the advisers and personnel that Business Link retains to service its clients (Bennett et al. 2001).

Another approach is to look at the cost effectiveness of an intervention. In the case of a measure designed to increase employment, cost per job estimates might be provided. Such an approach, if carefully undertaken, can enable comparisons to be made across measures in order to answer questions like 'What is the cheapest way of creating x jobs?' Its limitation of course is that while the costs side is quantified in monetary terms, the benefits side is not. Thus no judgement can be made from the evaluation about the 'worthwhileness' of the intervention.

The most comprehensive kind of evaluation, however, examines both costs and benefits in monetary terms. This then permits a rate of return to be calculated. The critical issue here is the clear definition of the entity incurring the costs and receiving the benefits. It might be the public purse, with revenues (inflows) being set against expenditures (outflows). A similar exercise might be done for the particular agency responsible for the measure. A broader perspective might be taken, and the entity defined as society at large. In this case, a social cost benefit analysis is the corresponding evaluation tool. In principle such analysis seeks to evaluate all the costs and benefits that arise as the result of an intervention although in practice this is rarely possible.

An early example of a cost benefit study of a small firms policy intervention was carried out by Johnson and Thomas (1984). They found a very high rate of return for a government financed training programme designed to help fifteen would-be founders set up in business. Interestingly, they also found that most of the benefits were generated by only a handful of trainees: two businesses generated over 70 per cent of the benefits of the programme which covered all of its costs. However it is not at all clear that these high fliers could have been identified *prior to* the programme; thus part of the inevitable cost of training these people may be the training of those who decide, in the end, not to go into business or who end up as 'low fliers'.

Evaluation: some issues

There are three thorny issues that are common to many different types of evaluation. The first concerns the measurement of *the difference* that an intervention makes to the recipient and his or her business. Some estimate needs to be made of what the situation would have been like in the absence of the policy. 'Before and after' studies and the use of control groups are two possible options that may be employed to get a handle on the 'without policy' position (or the 'counterfactual' as it is sometimes called). These kinds of approach enable estimates to be made of a policy's deadweight, i.e. the extent to which the observed 'outcomes' would have happened anyway.

The second issue is the 'knock-on' effects generated by a policy intervention. Most attention has been paid here to the displacement caused by competitive forces. The policy-induced development of the recipient firm(s) may lead to *other* firms experiencing a downturn in their business as a result of the increased competition. This adverse effect needs to be incorporated into any evaluation to avoid the overestimation of the benefits of the policy. However, the impact may not only be adverse. There may be *positive* knock-on effects. Some possibilities have already alluded to earlier in this chapter.

There may sometimes be unanticipated side-effects. For example, the exemptions given to small firms under certain regulations may affect their behaviour. A study in Italy (Schivardi and Torrini 2005) has looked at the impact of exemption for small firms from employment protection legislation (EPL) on their growth pattern. It found that the existence of a threshold size (beyond which the EPL becomes effective) – fifteen employees in Italy – *reduced* the propensity of firms below that threshold to grow, albeit to a modest extent. Similarly, in the United Kingdom, a significant minority of firms may forgo growth in order to keep below the VAT threshold level (see the evidence reviewed in Chittenden et al. 2002).

Third, decisions have to made on the 'boundaries' of any evaluation. For example, if the concern is with employment generation, what is the geographical area – the 'reference area' – within which the evaluation is to be carried out? The wider the area, the more complex the likely impact, once knock-on effects are taken into account.

In an ideal world it would be good to conduct an *ex ante* evaluation, i.e. before expenditure is committed. But there may be so many uncertainties that this might simply not be possible. Indeed the only way of exploring whether a policy is worthwhile may be to implement it and *then* to monitor the experience.

A case study in policy development

In this section, a case study of a particular policy initiative is considered. It concerns the targeting of the birth rate by an RDA as a means of raising entrepreneurial activity in a particular region of England, the North East. This region has had a relatively poor long run record on business formation (Johnson and Conway 1995). When the RDAs for the English Regions were set up at the end of the 1990s, they were asked by central government to include 'business formations and survival rates' as one of their core 'state of the region' indicators, and the 'number of business start-ups and survival rates' as an indicator of their activities.[3]

Some background

In its original (1999) strategy document the RDA for the North East, One NorthEast (ONE), responded to this guidance and used births as a percentage of the business stock in the North East as a quantitative target (it has since modified its stance: Johnson 2005). It accepted an explicit target to 'increase business start-ups to [the] UK average by 2010' (ONE 1999: 103). (Such a target, implicitly couched here by ONE in terms of *numbers*, is nevertheless meaningful only in terms of birth *rates*.) This birth rate target for the region was an expression of the RDA's wider commitment to building a 'new' entrepreneurial culture' in the region, and its assessment that

> The key to strengthening the Region's wealth creating capacity is to provide an environment in which entrepreneurs can run successful businesses . . . New businesses will be essential elements of the Region's clusters because they are often visionary and flexible in their thinking, management and marketing. They provide the mechanisms that create whole new industries. The Region must rediscover the spirit of enterprise . . .
>
> To do this, we must motivate those already in the Region to start new businesses and equip them with the skills to do so.
>
> (ONE 1999: 44)

A number of observations may be made on the choice of a birth rate target to achieve this objective. First, the precise way in which the birth rate is specified has important implications for the number of births required to ensure equality of rates between the North East and the United Kingdom as a whole. For example, with the business stock as the denominator in the birth rate (as in ONE 1999), the North East would have needed another 315 births to ensure equality with the United Kingdom. However if the adult population had been used as the denominator, it is estimated that nearly 3800 additional births would have been required (see Johnson 2005). Clearly the financial implications of providing support for business births is likely to vary hugely with the precise specification of the target.

Second, an equality target of the kind adopted by ONE is inevitably affected by other regions' policies. A number of RDAs also articulated explicit birth rate aspirations at the time that ONE published its original strategy. Even the South East Development Agency (SEDA), the region with one of the highest formation rates already, indicated that it was seeking a 'step change' in that rate (SEDA 1999: 15). Thus the target ONE set for the North East was by its nature likely to be a constantly moving one.

Third, predictions about the future time path of the measure specified by ONE in 1999 is complicated by the direct effect of an increase in the numerator on the denominator – more births imply an immediate increase in stock – and by any changes in the survival rate, of both new and existing firms, on the denominator. Births and deaths may not of course be independent. The former may for example stimulate deaths among the existing business stock, through a 'competition' effect. Alternatively, births may reduce deaths through a 'multiplier' effect. Births (deaths) may also affect births (deaths) in a subsequent period. The evidence on these relationships is mixed (Johnson and Parker 1994, 1996).

As far as the survival rate is concerned, it is worth noting that ONE also committed itself to raising the survival rate of new businesses to the UK average

(ONE 1999: 103). Paradoxically, an increased survival rate, which lowers the rate at which the stock is depleted, does of course make the attainment of the quantitative birth target specified in 1999 even more challenging.

Does it make sense to target the regional birth rate?

So far only technical issues of measurement have been considered. There are however more fundamental issues associated with a target that seeks to obtain equivalence in the birth rate between the North East and the United Kingdom and with having a specific set of policies designed to raise the birth rate to achieve this goal.

For example, while comparability with the United Kingdom is an understandable aim, there may be little reason to suppose that the North East's optimal rate, given its industrial structure, the available opportunities, the way those opportunities are perceived and the supply of would-be founders, should all be the same as elsewhere. In the absence of this similarity, the appropriate mix of new and existing business activity is likely to vary across regions.

A second issue of a fundamental kind relates to the complex set of environmental and other determinants that lie behind birth rates. Some of these have been explored in earlier chapters. Policy initiatives designed specifically to encourage births may succeed in compensating for factors in the economic environment that are less favourable to formation but there is likely to be a limit on the extent to which such compensation can be made. ONE of course was aware of the need for an altogether broader approach to the economic needs of the North East, but there are always dangers that the identification of a specific birth rate objective will distort policy priorities.

This example of policy targeting provides an ample illustration of the complexity of policymaking and the challenges faced by policymakers even in just one aspect of small firms activity, namely formation. It serves to emphasise the crucial importance of developing targets that are well thought through, the value of regular evaluation of those that are implemented and of course, a willingness to adapt targets in the light of experience.

Concluding comment

This chapter has demonstrated that the formulation, delivery and evaluation of policy towards small firms are complex matters. Real precision is needed in (for example) the development of target measures. Furthermore, simply because an effect can be shown – this is a difficult enough task in itself, given the need to have a counterfactual – does not of itself justify the investment of public funds, even where that effect in terms of (say) employment or profitability is large. By the same token, the existence of high cost levels does not necessarily mean that a policy is not worthwhile. Much can be done to assess the potential impact of a new policy before it is introduced, but it is unlikely that any firm assessment will be possible (if at all) until the policy has been up and running for some time. Thus significant risk is likely to be associated with any new initiative and some policies will inevitably be failures. This in turn highlights the need for rigorous evaluation procedures to be in place. There is much to be said too for evaluative work being undertaken by analysts who are independent of the policymakers.

10 Some implications for small business management

Introduction

This book has been primarily concerned with economic aspects of small business activity in advanced economies, notably the United Kingdom. Its main purpose has been to describe, analyse and understand such activity at a general level, to stand back and look at the overall picture. As a result of all the work that has been done on new and small firms, over the past few decades, much more is now known about the factors behind small firm formation, survival and growth, the economic role of small firms, their financing and the effects of policy intervention. However it is appropriate to ask how far this material is relevant for the individual who is thinking of setting up in business, or who is already established in business and thinking about the next move, or about how to run his or her business more effectively.

There is in fact an enormous how-to-do-it literature which seeks to provide help to individual owners of would-be or actual small businesses: in June 2006, Amazon's UK website listed 3900 titles under 'small business management'. The quality of this material is variable, with advice in the more popular manuals sometimes assuming self-evident truths about good practice, based on only a limited evidential base. As indicated above, the primary task of this book has not been to provide direct assistance to those in small business, even though there is clearly more that could be done in this area. But the question remains: does the material presented here have any practical value?

Perhaps one of the key contributions of this book, in terms of the actual management of small businesses, is the provision of a broader context for the activities of such businesses. Of course by the nature of things, specific implications for an individual business cannot be derived from a general picture. But an awareness of the wider context is important for a healthy small business, not least because it generates important questions and challenges. Some of the areas where this is the case are outlined below.

The large number of small businesses

The first (rather obvious) point that emerges from an analysis of the wider context is that there is a vast number of small businesses around and that they tend, not surprisingly, to be concentrated in sectors that are more conducive to small-scale activity. This in turn poses challenges to the small business person. Is there room for me? How can I compete effectively with those in the same line of business? Can I make my business sufficiently distinctive to give me a competitive edge? If I think I have spotted a market opportunity, how can I be sure that others have not spotted it too and are not planning to exploit it? Why should I be successful, when others are not?

Survival, growth and tubulence

The general evidence on survival, growth and turbulence is also instructive for small business owners. It is self-evident that some new firms become outstanding successes. A number become substantial market leaders, sometimes within a fairly short period of birth. Furthermore, alongside these spectacular successes, there are many firms that remain small but which provide an important economic function and a good living for their owners. Chapter 6 however showed that the majority of new firms have only a limited life span and that, of those who survive, few grow to any substantial size. Chapter 7 then highlighted the high levels of turbulence that exist, particularly in the smaller size bands: significant numbers of births and deaths, as well as substantial levels of expansion and contraction of existing firms, characterise the business scene, even over fairly short periods. This turbulence is a reflection of the dynamic, competitive nature of the business world which many new businesses enter. Such findings should inject a note of realism into plans for small-scale activity. Spectacular growth and market dominance are the exception rather than the rule. Would-be founders who have ambitious plans for growth or market dominance need to be clear as to why their venture would be sufficiently different from the overwhelming majority of new businesses to enable them to reach their goal. Even the founder with very modest ambitions is not immune from the challenge that the wider picture on survival and growth generates.

The need to be aware of this broader picture is reinforced by the suggestion, in Chapter 4, that new business founders tend to overestimate their early prospects. Without some optimism, little would be achieved, but at the same time, realistic awareness of the possible challenges and dangers is likely to be beneficial. At the every least, some explicit regard for the implications of unfulfilled expectations should be an important element in planning.

Market characteristics

Innovation

There are particular issues that arise out of the economic literature on small firms and innovation. Clearly, the relative advantage of small-scale operations in the innovative process varies from sector to sector. While it may be possible for a small business to innovate successfully in an industry where the technology tends to favour large firms – for example, because of the nature of the production process or heavy R&D costs – the likelihood is that the challenges will be severe. They need to be taken on with open eyes. Even where conditions are relatively favourable for small firms, the risk involved remains substantial. In this context it is worth stressing again the point made in Chapter 7 that while possession of a patent may be possible for a small business, its *defence* may not be.

Costs

Markets vary in their cost structures. In this context, the discussion in Chapter 2 of the concept of minimum efficient scale, including the *shape* of the long run average cost schedule that defines it, is a powerful one. It highlights the importance of operating at an appropriate level and the cost disadvantages that flow from a departure from that level. Clearly these disadvantages – and the implications for business competitiveness and viability – will vary from sector to sector.

In reality, the concept of MES is a messy one and measurement is sometimes problematic. Nevertheless it does pose fundamentally significant questions for the small business operator. First, what is the most efficient scale of operation for the market in which I am operating? And secondly, if I depart from that scale, what will be the cost penalties? And how long would it take me to grow to the optimum? Of course, some small businesses may be seeking to *change* the relevant MES through innovation or they may explore ways in which cost disadvantages may be minimised. They may also seek to develop a market niche where their customers will be willing to pay for the cost disadvantages that small-scale production generates because they are receiving other benefits such as personalised service. For the general run of businesses however, MES will be an important determinant of viability, especially in a competitive market.

Growth

In Chapter 5 it was shown that a new firm is more likely to survive and develop in a growing market. It is important therefore for the small business owner to look at what is happening, *as a whole*, to the market that he or she is in. This in turn raises difficult questions about how the appropriate market should be defined. Is it local or national? And what is the relevant range of products or services that defines it? Although these questions are not easy to answer, the very process of addressing them is likely to have a clarifying effect on the nature of the competition that the business faces.

When looking at the growth of a market, it is important too to have an eye to what is happening more generally in the area or region in which the firm is located. Chapter 6 showed that, for a whole range of reasons, including differences in the level of demand for the products and services of small businesses, regions differ markedly in their rates of business formation, and this variation is almost certainly reflected in small business activity as whole. No one business is going to be able singlehandedly to alter the underlying conditions that give rise to these differences.

Entrepreneurial activity

In Chapter 3, the multifaceted nature of the entrepreneurial function was emphasised. Against this background, it is helpful for small business owners to be aware of the particular skills and abilities that they bring to their activities and of the areas where others are needed to complement what they have to offer. For example, some owners may be particularly strong on generating innovative ideas, yet be less good at evaluating these ideas realistically in commercial terms or at implementing them. In this kind of situation they need to look for ways in which they can expand, formally or informally, their skills portfolio.

There are particular issues arising out of Kirzner's notion of entrepreneurial alertness. This notion is, for example, particularly valuable in highlighting the importance, for commercial success, of maintaining property rights in market insights. It also encourages would-be and existing owners to be on the look out for new market opportunities.

Family issues

Many small businesses draw heavily on family resources, in terms of both finance and labour to enable them to grow. The discussion of intergenerational transfers of family businesses in Chapter 7 raises issues important questions about how such businesses can be passed on successfully to the next generation, a process that takes careful planning and skill.

Finance

A key area for small business is of course finance. Chapter 8 outlined some significant characteristics of the structure of small business finance and the implications of these characteristics for small business management. A critical challenge here is the trade-off that may exist between the objectives and preferences of the owner and the funding available. If for example the owner does not wish to reduce his or her control over the business, then this will in turn limit the owner's financial options for external finance. Particular challenges are likely to arise for new or early stage businesses, where there is no track record and for business in high tech areas where the risks may be high.

Policy

Chapter 9 on policy issues provided a number of economic grounds for the public support of small business. The discussion in this chapter is most relevant for those small business owners and groups who lobby for more assistance to small businesses. It suggests that where there are no or only weak political imperatives driving policy, the case for policy support is likely to be stronger if it can be convincingly argued not only that in the absence of assistance, some outcome would not be forthcoming, but also that the outcome would generate important public benefits that outweigh the costs.

Concluding comment

While this book has not sought to provide a manual for the management of small businesses, it does nevertheless offer some important food for thought to the would-be or actual small business owner. How such owners respond to the challenges of the wider picture of small-scale operations that have been presented in this book is likely to be a significant determinant, alongside other factors, of how successful they will prove to be.

Notes

1 Introduction

1 As always, there are exceptions: for example, see Steindl (1945) for a treatment of small firms that was well ahead of its time.
2 A complete list of these collections would be lengthy. However, key ones are Casson (1990); Acs (1996); Sexton and Landstrom (2000); Storey (2000); Acs and Audretsch (2003); Parker (2006).

2 Why study small firms?

1 Europe-19 is defined here as the EU-15, plus Iceland, Norway and Switzerland including Liechtenstein.
2 The European Commission estimated that in 2003, there were about 2.2 million enterprises in the United Kingdom with under 50 employees in the non-primary sectors (European Commission 2004: 77). This compares with the UK Small Business Service estimate for the same year of just under 4 million in this size category for all industries, except agriculture, hunting, forestry and fishing (www.sbs.gov.uk).
3 For a good review of some key issues in this literature, see Dietrich (1994).
4 For an example, see Johnson (1986: 9).
5 In the Bolton Committee's *terms of reference*, small firms were broadly defined as firms of under 200 employees.
6 See *Official Journal of the European Communities*, L107, 1996, 39 (30 April).
7 Elasticity here simply measures the responsiveness of the small firm share in a sector to a change in the relevant variable, e.g. capital intensity, in that sector. More formally, it is the proportionate change in the small firm share divided by the proportionate change in the variable.
8 For their employment data, Brock and Evans (1986) excluded construction.
9 Of course the quality of the managing director required will vary depending on the size of the firm. But there are likely to be substantial ranges of output over which broadly the same quality of person will be appropriate.

3 The entrepreneurial function

1 For example, Audretsch (1999: 1) defines entrepreneurship as the 'process by which new people start and expand new firms'. Lazear (2002) adopts a similar approach.

2 Considerable care needs to be exercised here. For example, in their important article, Low and MacMillan (1988) proposed that entrepreneurship should be defined in terms of 'the creation of new enterprise', but 'new enterprise' does of course have a wider connotation than simply the setting up of a brand new business entity.

3 For a more rounded view of the nature of entrepreneurship, see the special issue of *Entrepreneurship Theory and Practice*, 2001, 25(4).

4 Casson's (1999: 45) assessment is stark: 'The recent revival of interest in entrepreneurship owes almost nothing to the intellectual initiative of economists'.

5 As Blaug (1995: 10) suggests, entrepreneurship and the standard neoclassical theory of the firm are basically incompatible. See also Barreto (1989: 132–3) quoted in Blaug (1995). It is worth noting that in the mid-1990s one of the leading elementary textbooks on economics – Parkin and King (1995) – contained *no* reference to the entrepreneur in its index. Significantly perhaps, the third edition (Parkin et al. 1997) *does* have such a reference.

6 The development of the economics of search has greatly enriched the theoretical treatment of the behaviour of economic actors, by incorporating the presence of uncertainty, but even here, the information that is being sought is known to be available. There is little room for what Kirzner (1997) calls 'unknown ignorance'.

7 The term 'entrepreneur' had been used before Cantillon. For example, in France, by the early sixteenth century, leaders of military expeditions were being referred to as entrepreneurs. In the early eighteenth century the term was often used by the French to describe government road, bridge, harbour and fortification contractors. See Cochran (1968); see also Kirzner (1979: 38).

8 It is interesting to note that de Belidor, writing at roughly the same time as Cantillon, envisaged the entrepreneur as *selling* at a *certain* price, agreed for a public works contract, but as being *uncertain*, at the time of that contract, about the costs that would have to be incurred to fulfil it. This is the opposite of Cantillon's description of the entrepreneur's activity, but it has the same effect of generating a residual. See Hoselitz (1951).

9 Or 'undertakers' as the English translation has it.

10 Knight (1921: 289 n) makes just this point.

11 There were of course other writers prior to Say who emphasised the planning and organising role of the entrepreneur, but as Hébert and Link (1982: 30) point out, currency in the use of a term does not indicate 'intellectual lineage'. This undoubtedly lies with Say.

12 Schumpeter (1934: 137) does however accept that an entrepreneur may risk his/her *reputation*. His point that entrepreneurs do not bear risk relates to the 'direct economic responsibility of failure' (1934: 137). He does not discuss the possibility that the entrepreneur is also risking his labour time.

13 It has already been pointed out that Schumpeter emphasised the importance of firms that are new (in an undefined way) in the innovation process, but even this view is consistent with industry variations which is the point being made here. A similar point may be made of Marshall's (1920: 263) 'trees of the forest' analogy: while the newer firm may typically be more vigorous than the older firm, the differences attributable to age are likely to vary with the industrial context.

14 Gibb (2002) has explored the implications of this wider vision for education and research. He has argued very persuasively that it is vitally important

to move the focus of entrepreneurship teaching and research away from the narrow business orientation towards the notion of the development of the enterprising person in a wide range of contexts and the design of organizations of all kinds to facilitate appropriate levels of 'effective' entrepreneurial behaviour.

(Gibb 2002: 258)

4 Setting up in business

1 The *GEM* project is an ongoing, international comparative study of entrepreneurial activity across a wide range of countries. For further details see www.gemcon sortium.org. The *GEM* project is unique in terms of its scale and coverage.
2 Supporting data are available from the author.
3 Specifically, those self-employed who are not in a family firm.
4 This is subtly different from a concern with the characteristics of those that move into self-employment in any given time period.
5 White males accounted for over three-quarters of the full-time self-employed in the United States in 1985 (Evans and Leighton 1989).
6 These authors however also show that IQ is not significant in the earnings equation for the self-employed. This in turn suggests that individuals with higher IQs become self-employed for reasons other than income.
7 For the self-employed generally, the score is negative, but statistically insignificant.
8 The higher this score, the lower the control that individuals perceive themselves to have over their own destiny.
9 This finding is derived as follows. Borjas and Bronars (1989) use their probit regression for Whites to predict what the self-employment rate for the other groups would be if the mechanism that determined the rates for Whites was also used to generate the self-employment rates for these groups. This procedure raises the rate for Blacks and Hispanics (to 10.5 and 12.0 per cent respectively) near to that of Whites. It also raises the Asian rate to a level (15.4 per cent) substantially *above* the White rate.
10 Bernhardt (1994) however shows that while married status is not significant in determining the self-employment propensity among white Canadian males, the presence of a *working* spouse (by 'working' Bernhardt presumably means 'in gainful employment') has a significant and positive effect.
11 This non-linearity is of course consistent with the Evans and Leighton (1989) finding on family net worth: see text.

5 Variations in formation activity

1 The UK data in Table 5.2B (bottom part), to be considered later in the text, yields a correlation between the two birth rates across regions of 0.78. The correlation between the two death rates is however a little higher at 0.84.
2 The correlation coefficient between the 2002 early-stage entrepreneurial rate (equivalent to what was called 'total entrepreneurial activity' in previous *GEM* reports), as measured in Table 5.1, and the self-employment rate provided in OECD (1998: 45) for the nineteen countries common to the two studies was 0.47.
3 Data collected by Barclays plc.

4 A broader population measure would not be meaningful in an industry context, whereas it would be when looking at *spatial* variations.

5 This approach rather assumes that the propensity to set up in industry x is limited to those employed in industry x. This is clearly a significant assumption. Fortunately, the evidence (Johnson and Cathcart 1979a) suggests that most people setting up in business were previously employed in the broad industrial sector in which they were previously employed. Care however has to be taken in interpreting even this finding, since it is specific to the economic conditions under which it was obtained. Presumably there would be a set of circumstances under which people from a particular 'source' would be attracted into another industry in order to set up. Also, there is likely to be more industrial 'cross over' the finer the industrial classification used.

6 Some businesses may be able to put off their demise almost indefinitely. The evidence suggests however that such 'eternal businesses' are a minority (see p. 64).

7 The author is grateful to Blackwell Publishing for permission to use this material.

8 Keeble and Walker (1994) found that population *density* also had a positive effect. One reason for this is that a small firm is more likely to be viable in a densely populated area, than in one where the demand is very thinly spread.

9 The presence of collateral may vary with the size of firm. Black et al. (1996) point out that 95 per cent of overdrafts above £20,000 in Cressy's study were fully collateralised.

10 A contrary result may be found in Beesley (1955).

11 Robson (1996b) does however present some tentative hypotheses. In relation to inflation for example, he suggests two hypotheses to support a negative effect on formation, while acknowledging that any 'clear-cut' predictions on the inflation–formation relationship are difficult to derive. The first of his hypotheses is that business confidence may be lowered by a rise in inflation, because would-be founders may take such a rise as signalling a subsequent tightening of macro policy. This plausible suggestion is not however supported by direct evidence. The second argument is that inflation may generate errors, by would-be founders and potential creditors, in the valuation of future cash flows which causes the rejection of potentially viable ventures. Again the underpinnings of this argument are not developed. Much surely will depend on whether the inflation rate is *predictable*.

6 Survival and growth

1 Most of these new firms were single establishments, although some were the headquarters of new multi-plant firms: see an earlier version of Audretsch (1995): Audretsch (1994). Those new establishments that were set up by existing firms were excluded.

2 Dunne et al.'s (1989) study covered plants first appearing in the database in 1967, 1972 or 1977.

3 For single unit plants (as opposed to plants in multi-plant firms) however, Dunne et al. (1989) found that the decline in failure with plant size was not monotonic.

4 Entry is used here in its broadest sense, although *de novo* firms are likely to be by far the biggest category in numerical terms.

5 The mean start-up size was 7.6 employees, which seems rather high. Even in manufacturing, most new firms are likely to start with only 1 or 2 employees.

6 Drawn from the US Small Business Administration's Small Business Data Base.

7 Birch defines a gazelle as a business that has a minimum of $100,000 turnover and manages to grow at least 20 per cent in revenues over a four-year period: see his interview in *Fortune Small Business*, 12 January 2002. On Birch's estimates, no more than 3 per cent of businesses qualify as gazelles on this definition (see www.fortune.com/fortune/small business).

8 See Ucbasaran et al. (2001: 59f) for a review of the way in which researchers have sought to categorise small business owners.

9 According to a press release from the Department for Trade and Industry, 25 August 2005 (URN 05/92), only 0.1 per cent of business enterprises had 250 employees or more in 2004. Clearly the percentage would be less for enterprises with 500 or more employees.

10 Around the £4 million mark.

7 The economic role of small firms

1 The net job creation rate is in fact negative in all size bands, when the end year is used as a base. When the base year is used, this rate is positive for the two smallest size bands and then turns negative.

2 Includes identity, occupation and location (Brown et al. 1990: 36–7).

3 Such strategies would involve the payment of higher remuneration to persuade employees not to become union members.

4 In the work reviewed by Brown et al. (1990), this dividing line varies, and in some cases, is not specified.

5 Of course there are florist and jewellery chains which are able to take advantage of buying, marketing and other economies. But these advantages may be offset by the fact that such chains may not be able to offer the kind of service sought by some customers.

6 Hall (1997) has provided some evidence on some very long-lived companies that have been able to survive. He examined a sample of companies that had been trading before 1800 and were still in existence in the mid-1990s. (He traced 214 British companies that came into this category.) Many of them were still in their original industries, where the original product concept had maintained its currency. Interestingly he did not find that any particular way of managing dominated these companies. He does suggest though that they tend to go for underlying financial strength rather than profitability or growth; and that they tend to adopt a tolerant management style, which is accommodating towards dissent.

7 In this respect it should be noted that there is some evidence to suggest that in high income economies, there is a shift towards smaller scale activity (see Acs et al. 2005: 41). In this sense it is income growth that is causing the shift to smaller scale activity rather than the other way round.

8 Finance

1 Monetary financial institutions sterling net lending, seasonally adjusted. Data are taken from the Bank of England's statistical database (http://www.bankofengland. co.uk/statistics).

2 The relevant *Business Monitor* (MA3: *Company Finance*) ceased after publication of the 1990 figures (Central Statistical Office 1992).

3 Specifically, that the banks should be prepared where appropriate to offer term loan facilities in place of overdrafts; that the top limit on ICFC finance should be raised; and that there should be a new institution specifically designed to assist in the financing of technological innovation in small firms.

4 It may of course be possible to conceive of circumstances where the market may not clear in any period because of market inflexibilities. As a result, price may not move to its equilibrium level, r_e. and may remain (say) at r_1 in Figure 8.1. The resultant 'gap', measured at r_1 and which is solely the result of the market failing to clear, may be measured in one of two ways: as $F_2 - F_1$, the gap at the prevailing out-of-equilibrium price, r_1, or as $F_2 - F_e$, the difference between what is demanded at r_1 and what would be supplied at the equilibrium price, r_e. This gap would of course be removed by the market moving to r_e. This option is not treated explicitly in the text as it is not really compatible with the notion of a competitive market.

5 In January 2006, the Office of Fair Trading announced a review of these undertakings.

6 As Mason and Harrison (2000) point out, this estimate is crucially dependent on assumptions about the proportion of business angels who are members of business angel networks. A doubling of this proportion would result in a doubling of the figures in the text.

9 Issues in policy

1 This directory may be viewed at http://www.businesslink.gov.uk (accessed 28 April 2006).

2 In one of their articles Robson and Bennett (2000) suggest that if anything, the relationship is negative, i.e. poor growth and performance is associated with Business Link usage. One interpretation of this result is that Business Link is being used by firms who want to stem actual or potential decline rather than as a means of enhancing growth.

3 It is puzzling why *numbers* should be used for business start-ups and *rates* for measuring survival.

References

Acs, Z.J. (ed.) (1996) *Small Firms and Economic Growth*, International Library of Critical Writings in Economics no. 61, Cheltenham: Edward Elgar.

Acs, Z.J. and Audretsch, D.B. (1988) 'Innovation in large and small firms: an empirical analysis', *American Economic Review*, 78: 678–90.

Acs, Z.J. and Audretsch, D.B. (1990) *Innovation and Small Firms*, Cambridge, MA: MIT Press.

Acs, Z.J. and Audretsch, D.B. (eds) (2003) *Handbook of Entrepreneurship Research: An Interdisciplinary Survey and Introduction*, Boston, MA: Kluwer Academic.

Acs, Z.J., Audretsch, D.B. and Evans, D.S. (1994) *Why does the Self-Employment Rate Vary across Countries and Over-Time?* Centre for Economic Policy Research (CEPR) Discussion Paper, no. 871, London: CEPR.

Acs, Z.J., Carlsson, B. and Karlsson, C. (1999) 'The linkages among entrepreneurship, SMEs and the macroeconomy', in Z.J. Acs, B. Carlsson and C. Karlsson (eds) *Entrepreneurship, Small and Medium-sized Enterprises and the Macroeconomy*, Cambridge: Cambridge University Press.

Acs, Z.J., Arenius, P., Hay, M. and Minniti, M. (2005) *Global Entrepreneurship Monitor 2004 Executive Report*, Babson Park, MA: Babson College and London: London Business School.

Armington, C. and Acs, Z. (2002) 'The determinants of regional variation in new firm formation', *Regional Studies*, 36: 33–45.

Armington, C. and Odle, M. (1982) 'Small business: how many jobs?', *Brookings Review*, Winter: 14–17.

Ashworth, J.S., Johnson, P.S. and Conway, C. (1998) 'How good are small firms at predicting employment?', *Small Business Economics*, 10: 379–87.

Aston Business School (1991) *Constraints on the Growth of Small Firms: A Report on a Survey of Small Firms*, London: DTI.

Atkinson, J. and Hurstfield, J. (2004) *Small Business Service. Annual Survey of Small Businesses: UK 2003*, prepared by the Institute for Employment Studies, London: Small Business Service.

Audretsch, D.B. (1994) 'Innovation, survival and growth', paper presented at a Conference on the Post Entry Performance of Firms, Lisbon, 27–28 May.

Audretsch, D.B. (1995) 'Innovation, growth and survival', *International Journal of Industrial Organization*, 13: 441–57.

Audretsch, D.B. (1999) 'Linking entrepreneurship to economic growth', in G.D. Libecap (ed.) *The Sources of Entrepreneurial Activity*, vol. 11, *Advances in the Study of Entrepreneurship, Innovation and Economic Growth*, Stamford, CT: JAI Press.

Audretsch, D.B. (2002) *Entrepreneurship: a Survey of the Literature*, a report prepared for the European Commission (Enterprise Directorate General), Bloomington, IN: Institute for Development Strategies, Indiana University and London: Centre for Economic Policy Research.

Audretsch, D.B. and Fritsch, M. (2002) 'Growth regimes over time and space', *Regional Studies*, 36: 113–24.

Bank of England (1996) *The Financing of Technology-Based Small Firms*, London: Bank of England.

Bank of England (2001) *The Financing of Technology-Based Small Firms*, London: Bank of England.

Bank of England (2004) *Finance for Small Firms – An Eleventh Report*, London: Bank of England.

Barkham, R. (1992) 'Regional variations in entrepreneurship: some evidence from the United Kingdom', *Entrepreneurship and Regional Development*, 4: 225–44.

Barreto, H. (1989) *The Entrepreneur in Microeconomic Theory: Disappearance and Explanation*, London: Routledge.

Baumol, W. (1982) 'Contestable markets: an uprising in the theory of industrial structure', *American Economic Review*, 72: 1–15.

Beesley, M. (1955) 'The birth and death of industrial establishments: experience in the West Midlands conurbation', *Journal of Industrial Economics*, 4: 45–61.

Beesley, M. and Hamilton, R. (1984) 'Small firms' seedbed role and the concept of turbulence', *Journal of Industrial Economics*, 33: 217–31.

Bennett, R. and Robson, P. (1999) 'Business Link: use, satisfaction and comparison with Business Shop and Business Connect', *Policy Studies*, 20: 107–31.

Bennett, R. and Robson, P. (2003) 'Use, satisfaction and the influence of local governance regime', *Policy Studies*, 24: 163–86.

Bennett, R.J., Robson, P.J.A. and Bratton, W.J.A. (2001) 'Government advice networks for SMEs: an assessment of the influence of local context on Business Link use, impact and satisfaction', *Applied Economics*, 33: 871–85.

Bernhardt, I. (1994) 'Comparative advantage in self-employment and paid work', *Canadian Journal of Economics*, 27: 273–89.

Birch, D. (1979) *The Job Generation Process*, Cambridge, MA: MIT Program on Neighborhood and Regional Change, no. 14.

Birley, S. (1986) 'Succession in the family firm: the inheritor's view', *Journal of Small Business Management*, 24: 36–43.

Black, J., de Meza, D. and Jeffreys, D. (1996) 'House prices, the supply of collateral and the enterprise economy', *Economic Journal*, 106: 60–75.

Blanchflower, D.G. and Oswald, A.J. (1991) *What Makes an Entrepreneur?*, NBER Working Paper no. 3252 (revised), Washington, DC: National Bureau of Economic Research.

Blaug, M. (1995) *Entrepreneurship in the History of Economic Thought*, Discussion Paper in Economics no. 95/15, Exeter: University of Exeter.

Bolton Committee (1971) *Report of the Committee of Inquiry on Small Firms*, (Bolton Committee Report), Cmnd 4811, London: HMSO.

Borjas, G.J. (1986) 'The self-employment experience of immigrants', *Journal of Human Resources*, 21: 485–506.

Borjas, G.J. and Bronars, S.G. (1989) 'Consumer discrimination and self-employment', *Journal of Political Economy*, 97: 581–605.

British Venture Capital Association (BVCA) (2004) *BVCA Report on Investment Activity 2003*: http://www.bvca.co.uk.

Brock, W.A. and Evans, D.S. (1986) *The Economics of Small Businesses*, New York: Holmes and Meier.

Brown, C., Hamilton, J. and Medoff, J. (1990) *Employers Large and Small*, Cambridge, MA: Harvard University Press.

Bryson, J.R., Daniels, P.W. and Ingram, D.R. (1999) 'Evaluating the impact of business link on the performance and profitability of SMEs in the United Kingdom', *Policy Studies*, 20: 95–105.

Burns, P. (2007) *Entrepreneurship and Small Business*, 2nd edn, Basingstoke: Palgrave.

Cantillon, R. (1931) *Essay on the Nature of Commerce in General*, 1755 trans. and edited by H. Higgs, 1931, reissued 1959, London: Royal Economic Society and Frank Cass.

Carree, M. and Klomp, L. (1996) 'Small businesss and job creation: a comment', *Small Business Economics*, 8: 317–22.

Casson, M. (ed.) (1990) *Entrepreneurship*, International Library of Critical Writings in Economics no. 3, Aldershot: Edward Elgar.

Casson, M. (1999) 'Entrepreneurship and the theory of the firm', in Z.J. Acs, B. Carlsson and C. Karlsson (eds) *Entrepreneurship, Small and Medium-sized Enterprises and the Macroeconomy*, Cambridge: Cambridge University Press.

Casson, M. (2003) *The Entrepreneur: An Economic Theory*, 2nd edn, Cheltenham: Edward Elgar.

Caves, R. E. (1998) 'Industrial organization and new findings on the turnover and mobility of firms', *Journal of Economic Literature*, 36: 1947–982.

Central Statistical Office (1992) *Business Monitor: Company Finance*, MA3, 23rd issue, London: Central Statistical Office.

Chittenden, F., Kauser, S. and Potzouris, P. (2002) *Regulatory Burdens of Small Business: A Literature Review*, a research project funded by the Small Business Service and supported by the Leverhulme Trust: http://www.sbs.gov.uk/SBS_Gov_files/researchandstats/Regulation-Report.pdf

Churchill, N.C. and Lewis, V.L. (1983) 'The five stages of small business growth', *Harvard Business Review*, 61: 30–50.

Cochran, T.C. (1968) 'Entrepreneurship', in D. Sills (ed.) *International Encyclopaedia of the Social Sciences*, vol. 5: 87–90, New York: Macmillan and Free Press.

Commission of the European Communities (1990) *Enterprises in the European Community*, Brussels: Office for Official Publications of the European Communities.

Competition Commission (2002) *The Supply of Banking Services by Clearing Banks to Small and Medium-sized Enterprises. Vol. 1: Summary and Conclusions*, Cm 5319, London: Competition Commission.

Cooper, C., Woo, C.Y. and Dunkelberg, W.C. (1988) 'Entrepreneurs' perceived chances for success', *Journal of Business Venturing*, 3: 97–108.

Cosh, A. and Hughes, A. (1994) 'Size, financial structure and profitability: UK companies in the 1980s', in A. Hughes and D.J. Storey (eds) *Finance and the Small Firm*, London: Routledge.

Cosh, A. and Hughes, A. (2000a) 'CEOs, management structure, growth objectives and constraints', in A. Cosh and A. Hughes (eds) *British Enterprise in Transition*, Cambridge: ESRC Centre for Business Research.

Cosh, A. and Hughes, A. (2000b) 'Profitability and finance in SMEs', in A. Cosh and A. Hughes (eds) *British Enterprise in Transition*, Cambridge: ESRC Centre for Business Research.

Cowling, M. and Taylor, M. (2001) 'Entrepreneurial women and men: two different species?', *Small Business Economics*, 16: 167–75.

Creedy, J. and Johnson, P.S. (1983) 'Firm formation in manufacturing', *Applied Economics*, 15: 177–85.

Curran, J. and Blackburn, A. (2001) *Researching the Small Enterprise*, London: Sage.

Dale, I. and Morgan, A. (2001) 'Job creation: the role of new and small firms', Sheffield: Small Business Service and Newcastle: Trends Business Research.

Daly, M. (1990) 'The 1980s: a decade of growth in enterprise', *Employment Gazette*, 98: 553–65.

Daly, M., Campbell, M., Robson, G. and Gallagher, G. (1991) 'Job creation 1987–9: the contributions of small and large firms', *Employment Gazette*, 99: 589–96.

Davidsson, P. (2005) 'Developments in the study of nascent entrepreneurs', paper given at the Conference on Nascent Entrepreneurship: the Hidden Potential, Durham, UK, September.

Davidsson, P. and Wiklund, J. (2001) 'Levels of analysis in entrepreneurship research: current research practice and suggestions for the future', *Entrepreneurship Theory and Practice*, 25: 81–99.

Davis, S.J., Haltiwanger, J. and Schuh, S. (1996) 'Small business and job creation: dissecting the myth and reassessing the facts', *Small Business Economics*, 8: 297–315.

Dawson, M.W. (1996) *Small Firm Formation and Regional Economic Development*, London: Routledge.

Deakins, D. and Hussain, G. (1993) 'Overcoming the adverse selection problem: evidence and policy implications from a study of bank managers on the importance of different criteria used in making a lending decision', in F. Chittenden, M. Robertson and D. Watkins (eds) *Small Firms: Recession and Recovery*, London: Paul Chapman.

Department of Trade and Industry (2004a) *Companies in 2003–2004. Report for the Year Ended 31 March 2004*, London: The Stationery Office.

Department of Trade and Industry (2004b) *Passing the Baton – Encouraging Successful Business Transfers: Evidence and Key Stakeholder Opinion*, London: Small Business Service.

Department of Trade and Industry (2005) *Statistical Press Release. Business Start-ups and Closures: VAT Registrations and De-registrations in 2004*, URN 05/111 12 October 2005, London: DTI.

De Wit, G. and Van Winden, F.A.A.M. (1989) 'An empirical analysis of self-employment in the Netherlands', *Small Business Economics*, 1: 263–72.

Dietrich, M. (1994) *Transaction Cost Economics and Beyond*, London: Routledge.

Dobson, S. and Gerrard, B. (1989) 'Growth and profitability in the Leeds engineering sector', *Scottish Journal of Political Economy*, 36: 334–51.

Duncan, J.W. and Handler, D.P. (1994) 'The misunderstood role of business', *Business Economics*, 29: 7–13.

Dunne, P. and Hughes, A. (1994) 'Age, size, growth and survival: UK companies in the 1980s', *Journal of Industrial Economics*, 42: 115–40.

Dunne, T., Roberts, M.J. and Samuelson, L. (1989) 'The growth and failure of US manufacturing plants', *Quarterly Journal of Economics*, 104: 671–97.

European Commission (2004) *SMEs in Europe 2003*, Observatory of European SMEs 2003, no. 7, report submitted to the Enterprise Directorate General by KPMG Special Services, EIM Business and Policy Research and ENSR, Brussels, Luxembourg: Office for Official Publications of the European Communities.

Evans, D.S. (1987) 'The relationship between firm growth, size and age: estimates for 100 manufacturing industries', *Journal of Industrial Economics*, 35: 567–81.

Evans, D.S. and Leighton, L.S. (1989) 'Some empirical aspects of entrepreneurship', *American Economic Review*, 79: 519–35.

Evans, M.R.D. (1989) 'Immigrant entrepreneurship: effects of ethnic market size and isolated labour pool', *American Sociological Review*, 54: 950–62.

Freeman, C. and Soete, L. (1997) *The Economics of Industrial Innovation*, 3rd edn, London: Pinter.

Galbraith, J.K. (1956) *American Capitalism: The Concept of Countervailing Power*, revd edn, Boston, MA: Houghton Mifflin.

Ganguly, P. (1985) *UK Small Business Statistics and International Comparisons*, edited by Graham Bannock, published on behalf of the Small Business Research Trust, London: Harper and Row.

Geroski, P. (1991) *Market Dynamics and Entry*, Oxford: Blackwell.

Geroski, P. (1995) 'What do we know about entry?', *International Journal of Industrial Organization*, 13: 421–40.

Gibb, A. (2002) 'In pursuit of a new "enterprise" and "entrepreneurship" paradigm for learning: creative destruction, new values, new ways of doing things and new combinations of knowledge', *International Journal of Management Reviews*, 4: 233–69.

Gibrat, R. (1931) *Les Inégalités économiques*, Paris: Sirey.

Grilo, I. and Thurik, R. (2005) 'Determinants of entrepreneurial engagement levels in Europe and the US', paper given at the Conference on Nascent Entrepreneurship: the Hidden Potential', Durham, UK, September.

Gudgin, G. and Fothergill, S. (1984) 'Geographical variation in the rate of formation of new manufacturing plants', *Regional Studies*, 18: 203–6.

Hakim, C. (1989) 'Identifying fast growth small firms', *Employment Gazette*, 97: 29–41.

Hall, R. (1997) 'Long term survivors', *Journal of General Management*, 22: 1–15.

Hébert, R.F and Link, A.N. (1982) *The Entrepreneur: Mainstream Views and Radical Critiques*, New York: Praeger.

Hillier, B. and Ibrahimo, M.V. (1993) 'Asymmetric information and models of credit rationing', *Bulletin of Economic Research*, 45: 271–304.

HM Treasury (2004a) *Graham Review of the Small Firms Loan Guarantee: Interim Report*, London: HM Treasury.

HM Treasury (2004b) *Graham Review of the Small Firms Loan Guarantee: Recommendations*, London: HM Treasury.

HM Treasury and Small Business Service (2002a) *Cross Cutting Review of Government Services for Small Business*, available at: http://www.sbs.gov.uk/content/crosscutting/ccr_finalreport.pdf.

HM Treasury and Small Business Service (2002b) *Enterprise Britain: A Modern Approach to Meeting the Enterprise Challenge*, London: HMSO.

Hoselitz, B.F. (1951) 'The early history of entrepreneurial theory', *Explorations in Entrepreneurial History*, (series 1) 3: 193–200.

Jewkes, J., Sawers, D. and Stillerman, R. (1969) *The Sources of Invention*, 2nd edn, London: Macmillan.

Joel Popkin and Company (1997) *Small Business Share of Private, Nonfarm Gross Produc,* report prepared for the United States Small Business Administration (SBA), Office of Advocacy, Washington, DC: SBA.

Johnson, P.S. (1978) 'Policies towards small firms: time for caution?', *Lloyds Bank Review*, 129: 1–11.

Johnson, P.S. (1983) 'New manufacturing firms in the UK regions', *Scottish Journal of Political Economy*, 30: 75–9.

Johnson, P.S. (1986) *New Firms: An Economic Perspective*, London: Unwin Hyman.

Johnson, P.S. (2004) 'Differences in regional firm formation rates: a decomposition analysis', *Entrepreneurship Theory and Practice*, 28: 431–45 (Blackwell Publishing: see note 7, p. 137).

Johnson, P.S. (2005) 'Targeting firm births and economic regeneration in a lagging region', *Small Business Economics*, 24: 451–64.

Johnson, P.S. and Apps, R. (1979) 'Interlocking directorates among the UK's largest companies', *Antitrust Bulletin*, 24: 357–69.

Johnson, P.S. and Cathcart, D.G. (1979a) 'New manufacturing firms and regional development: some evidence from the Northern Region', *Regional Studies*, 13: 269–80.

Johnson, P.S. and Cathcart, D.G. (1979b) 'The founders of new manufacturing firms: a note on the size of their incubator plants', *Journal of Industrial Economics*, 28: 219–24.

Johnson, P.S. and Conway, C. (1995) 'Entrepreneurship and new firm formation', in L. Evans, P. Johnson, and B. Thomas (eds) *The Northern Region Economy. Progress and Prospects in the North of England*. London: Mansell.

Johnson, P.S. and Conway, C. (1996) 'Business entry, economic development and market competition: some evidence from the the Northern Region of the UK', Department of Economics, University of Durham, revised version of a paper given at the Conference on Monopoly and Competition, Polish Academy of Sciences, Warsaw, October 1995.

Johnson, P.S. and Conway, C. (1997) 'How good are the UK VAT registration data at measuring firm births?' *Small Business Economics*, 9: 403–9.

Johnson, P.S. and Parker, S. (1994) 'The interrelationships between births and deaths', *Small Business Economics*, 6: 283–90.

Johnson, P.S. and Parker, S. (1996) 'Spatial variations in the determinants and effects of firm births and deaths', *Regional Studies*, 30: 679–88.

Johnson, P.S. and Rodger, J. (1983) 'From redundancy to self-employment', *Employment Gazette*, 91: 260–4.

Johnson, P.S. and Thomas, R.B. (1984) 'Government policies towards business formation: an economic appraisal of a training scheme', *Scottish Journal of Political Economy*, 31: 131–46.

Johnson, P.S., Conway, C. and Kattuman, P. (1999) 'Small business growth in the short run', *Small Business Economics*, 12:103–12.

Jones, T., McEvoy, D. and Barrett, G. (1994) 'Raising capital for the ethnic minority small firm', in A. Hughes and D.J. Storey (eds) *Finance and the Small Firm*, London: Routledge.

Jovanovic, B. (1982) 'Selection and the evolution of industry', *Econometrica*, 50: 649–70.

Keeble, D. and Walker, S. (1994) 'New firms, small firms and dead firms: spatial patterns and determinants in the United Kingdom', *Regional Studies*, 28: 411–27.

Keeble, D., Walker, S. and Robson, M. (1993) *New Firm Formation and Small Business Growth in the UK*, research series no. 15, London: Employment Department.

Kingston University (2005) *Regulation and Small Firm Performance and Growth: a Review of the Literature*, mimeo, Kingston, UK: Small Business Centre.

Kirzner, I.M. (1973) *Competition and Entrepreneurship*, Chicago, IL: University of Chicago Press.

Kirzner, I.M. (1979) *Perception, Opportunity, and Profit: Studies in the Theory of Entrepreneurship*, Chicago, IL: University of Chicago Press.

Kirzner, I.M. (1985) *Discovery and the Capitalist Process*, Chicago, IL: University of Chicago Press.

Kirzner, I.M. (1997) 'Entrepreneurial discovery and the competitive market process: an Austrian approach', *Journal of Economic Literature*, 35: 60–85.

Knight, F.H. (1921) *Risk, Uncertainty, and Profit*, Boston, MA: Houghton Mifflin.

Koolman, G. (1971) 'Say's conception of the role of the entrepreneur', *Economica*, 38: 269–86.

Kwoka, J.E., Jr and White, L.J. (2001) 'The new industrial organization and small business', *Small Business Economics*, 16: 21–30.

Layard, P.R.G. (2005) *Happiness: Lessons from a New Science*, London: Allen Lane.

Lazear, E.P. (2002) *Entrepreneurship*, National Bureau of Economic Research (NBER), working paper 9109, Cambridge, MA: NBER.

Le, A.T. (1999) 'Empirical studies of self-employment', *Journal of Economic Surveys*, 13: 381–416.

Le Breton-Miller, I., Miller, D. and Steier, L.P. (2004) 'Towards an integrative model of effective FOB succession', *Entrepreneurship Theory and Practice*, 28: 305–28.

Loveman, G. and Sengenberger, W. (1991) 'The re-emergence of small-scale production: an international comparison', *Small Business Economics*, 3: 1–37.

Low, M.B. and MacMillan, I.C. (1988) 'Entrepreneurship – past research and future challenges', *Journal of Management*, 14: 139–61.

Lund, M. and Wright, J. (1999) 'The financing of small firms in the United Kingdom', *Bank of England Quarterly Bulletin*, May: 195–201.

Macmillan Committee (1931) *Report of the Committee on Finance and Industry* (Macmillan Committee Report), Cmd 3897, London: HMSO.

Marshall, A. (1920) *Principles of Economics*, 8th edn, reset 1949, London: Macmillan.

Mason, C.M. (1989) 'Explaining recent trends in new firm formation in the UK: some evidence from South Hampshire', *Regional Studies*, 23: 331–46.

Mason, C.M. and Harrison, R.T. (2000) 'The size of the informal venture capital market in the United Kingdom', *Small Business Economics*, 15: 137–48.

Mason, C.M. and Harrison, R.T. (2002a) 'Barriers to investment in the informal venture capital sector', *Entrepreneurship and Regional Development*, 14: 271–87.

Mason, C.M. and Harrison, R.T. (2002b) 'Is it worth it? The rates of return from informal venture capital investments', *Journal of Business Venturing*, 17: 211–36.

Mata, J. and Portugal, P. (1994) 'Life duration of new firms', *Journal of Industrial Economics*, 42: 227–43.

Minniti, M. (2006) 'Not for lack of trying: American entrepreneurship in black and white', paper given at the Conference on Nascent Entrepreneurship: the Hidden Potential, Durham, UK, September.

Minniti, M., Arenius, P. and Langowitz, N. (2005) *Global Entrepreneurship Monitor: 2004 Report on Women and Entrepreneurship*, Boston Park, MA: The Center for Women's Leadership, Babson College and London: London Business School.

Minniti, M. with Bygrave, W.D. and Autio, E. (2006) *Global Entrepreneurship Monitor. 2005 Executive Report*, Babson Park, MA: Babson College and London: London Business School.

Morrison, A., Breen, J. and Ali, S. (2003) 'Small business growth: intention, ability and opportunity', *Journal of Small Business Management*, 41: 417–25.

Mueller, P. (2005) 'Entrepreneurship in the region: breeding ground for nascent entrepreneurship?', paper given at the Conference on Nascent Entrepreneurship: the Hidden Potential, Durham, UK, September.

National Audit Office (2006) *Supporting Small Business*, HC 962 Session 2005–6, London: The Stationery Office.

OECD (1998) *Fostering Entrepreneurship*, Paris: OECD.

OECD (2005) *OECD SME and Entrepreneurship Outlook*, Paris: OECD.

Okolie, C. (2004) 'Why size class methodology matters in analyses of net and gross job flows', *Monthly Labor Review*, 127: 3–12.

ONE (1999) *Regional Economic Strategy for the North East: Unlocking our Potential.* Newcastle: One North East.

Oxenfeldt, A.R. (1943) *New Firms and Free Enterprise*, Washington, DC: American Council on Public Affairs.

Parker, S.C. (1999) 'The inequality of employment and self-employment incomes: a decomposition analysis for the U.K.', *Review of Income and Wealth*, 45: 263–74.

Parker, S.C. (2005) 'What happens to nascent entrepreneurs? An econometric analysis of the PSED', paper given at the Conference on Nascent Entrepreneurship: the Hidden Potential, Durham, UK, September.

Parker, S.C. (ed.) (2006) *The Economics of Entrepreneurship*, Cheltenham: Edward Elgar.

Parker, S.C. and Robson, M.T. (2004) 'Explaining international variations in self-employment: evidence from a panel of OECD countries, *Southern Economic Journal*, 71: 287–301.

Parkin, M. and King, D. (1995) *Economics*, 2nd edn, Wokingham, UK: Addison-Wesley.

Parkin, M., Powell, M. and Matthews, K. (1997) *Economics*, 3rd edn, Harlow: Addison-Wesley.

Pavitt, K., Robson, M. and Townsend, J. (1987) 'The size distribution of innovating firms in the UK: 1945–1983', *Journal of Industrial Economics*, 35: 297–316.

Penrose, E.T. (1980) *The Theory of the Growth of the Firm*, 2nd edn, Oxford: Basil Blackwell.

Radcliffe Committee (1958) *Committee on the Working of the Monetary System: Report* (Radcliffe Committee Report), Cmnd 827, London: HMSO.

Reid, G.C. (1993) *Small Business Enterprise: An Economic Analysis*. London: Routledge.

Reynolds, P., Storey, D. and Westhead, P. (1994) 'Cross-national comparisons of the variation in new firm formation rates', *Regional Studies*, 28: 443–56.

Reynolds, P.D., Bygrave, W. Autio, E. and others (2004) *Global Entrepreneurship Monitor 2003 Executive Report*, Babson Park, MA: Babson College, Kansas City, MO: Ewing Marion Kauffman Foundation and London: London Business School (see www.gemconsortium.org).

Robson, M.T. (1991) 'Self employment and new firm formation', *Scottish Journal of Political Economy*, 38: 352–68.

Robson, M.T. (1996a) 'Housing wealth, business creation and dissolution, in the U.K. regions', *Small Business Economics*, 8: 39–48.

Robson, M.T. (1996b) 'Macroeconomic factors in the birth and death of UK firms: evidence from quarterly VAT registrations', *Manchester School*, 43: 170–88.

Robson, P.J.A. and Bennett, R.J. (2000) 'SME growth: the relationship with business advice and external collaboration', *Small Business Economics*, 15: 193–208.

Say, J-B. (1880) *A Treatise on Political Economy or the Production, Distribution and Consumption of Wealth*, new American edn, based on a translation of the 4th edn of the French by C.R. Prinsep, with notes by the translator and a translation of the Introduction and additional notes by C.C. Biddle, 1880, rep. 1971, New York: Augustus M. Kelley.

Scherer, F.M. and Ross, D. (1990) *Industrial Market Structure and Economic Performance*, 3rd edn, Boston, MA: Houghton Mifflin.

Schivardi, F. and Torrini, R. (2005) *Identifying the Effects of Firing Restrictions through Size-Contingent Differences*, Centre for Economic Policy Research Discussion Paper no. 5303, London: CEPR.

Schultz, T.W. (1990) *Restoring Economic Equilibrium: Human Capital in the Modernizing Economy*, Oxford: Blackwell.

Schumpeter, J.A. (1934) *The Theory of Economic Development: An Inquiry into Profits, Capital, Credit, Interest, and the Business Cycle*, trans. Redvers Opie, first published as a Galaxy Book, 1961, New York: Oxford University Press.

Schumpeter, J.A. (1939) *Business Cycles: A Theoretical, Historical, and Statistical Analysis of the Capitalist Process*, vol. I, New York: McGraw-Hill.

Schumpeter, J.A. (1952) *Capitalism, Socialism and Democracy*, 5th edn, London: Allen and Unwin.

Scott, M. and Bruce, R. (1987) 'Five stages of growth in small business', *Long Range Planning*, 20: 45–52.

SEDA (1999) *Building a World Class Region: An Economic Strategy for the South East of England*. Guildford, UK: South East Development Agency.

Sexton, D.L. and Landstrom, H. (eds) (2000) *The Blackwell Handbook of Entrepreneurship*, Oxford: Blackwell.

Shane, S. and Venkataraman, S. (2000) 'The promise of of entrepreneurship as a field of research', *Academy of Management Review*, 25: 217–26.

Shepherd, D. (2003) 'Learning from business failure: propositions of grief recovery for the self-employed', *Academy of Management Review*, 28: 318–28.

Small Business Service (2005) *SME Statistics: Excel Files*, London: SBS (www.sbs.gov.uk).

Stam, E., Audtretsch, D. and Meijaaard, J. (2005) 'Renascent men or entrepreneurship as a one night stand', paper given at the Conference on Nascent Entrepreneurship: the Hidden Potential' Durham, UK, September.

Steindl, J. (1945) *Small and Big Business. Economic Problems of the Size of Firms*, Oxford University Institute of Statistics, Monograph 1, Oxford: Blackwell.

Stiglitz, J.E. and Weiss, A. (1981) 'Credit rationing in markets with imperfect information', *American Economic Review*, 71: 393–410.

Stone, I. (1992) *Restructuring of Manufacturing on Wearside: a Longer-term Perspective on Industrial Change*, research paper no 2, Newcastle: Newcastle Economics Research Unit.

Stoneman, P. (1995) 'Introduction', in P. Stoneman (ed.) *Handbook of the Economics of Innovation and Technological Change*, Oxford: Blackwell.

Storey, D. (1982) *Entrepreneurship and the New Firm*, London: Croom Helm.

Storey, D. (1991) 'The birth of new firms – does unemployment matter? A review of the evidence', *Small Business Economics*, 3: 167–78.

Storey, D. (1994) *Understanding the Small Business Sector*, London: Routledge.

Storey, D. (ed.) (2000) *Small Business: Critical Perspectives on Business and Management*, 4 vols, London: Routledge.

Storey, D. and Johnson, S. (1987) 'Regional variations in entrepreneurship in the UK', *Scottish Journal of Political Economy*, 34: 161–73.

Storey, D. and Jones, A.M. (1987) 'New firm formation: a labour market approach to industrial entry', *Scottish Journal of Political Economy*, 30: 37–51.

Thurik, A.R. (1999) 'Entrepreneurship, industrial transformation and growth', in G.D. Libecap (ed.) *The Sources of Entrepreneurial Activity*, vol. 11, *Advances in the Study of Entrepreneurship, Innovation and Economic Growth*, Stamford, CT: JAI Press.

Ucbasaran, D.P., Westhead, P. and Wright, M. (2001) 'The focus of entrepreneurial research: contextual and process issues', *Entrepreneurship Theory and Practice*, 25: 57–80.

von Thünen, J.H. (1960) *The Isolated State in Relation to Agriculture and Political Economy*, 1850, vol. 2, part 1, trans. B.W. Dempsey, in *The Frontier Wage*, Chicago, IL: Loyola University Press.

Weiss, L.W. (1991) *Structure, Conduct and Performance*, edited by D.B. Audretsch and H. Yamawaki, Hemel Hempstead: Harvester Wheatsheaf.

Westhead, P., Ucbasaran, P.D., Wright, M. and Binks, M. (2005) 'Novice, serial and portfolio entrepreneur behaviour and contributions', *Small Business Economics*, 25: 109–32.

White, L.J. (1981) *Measuring the Importance of Small Business in the American Economy*, Monograph Series in Finance and Economics. New York: Salomon Brothers Center for the study of Financial Institutions, Graduate School of Business Administration, New York University.

White, L.J. (1982) 'The determinants of the relative importance of small business', *Review of Economics and Statistics*, 64: 42–9.

Williams, B. (1994) *The Best Butter in the World*, London: Ebury Press.

Wilson Committee (1979) *The Financing of Small Firms: Interim Report of the Committee to Review the Functioning of Financial Institutions* (Wilson Committee Report), Cmnd 7503, London: HMSO.

Winter, S.G. (1984) 'Schumpeterian competition in alternative technological regimes', *Journal of Economic Behavior and Organization*, 5: 287–320.

Index